WHEN
IN
DOUBT,
MUMBLE

WHEN
IN
DOUBT,
MUMBLE

A Bureaucrat's
Handbook

James H. Boren

Introduction by
LAURENCE J. PETER
Hierarchiologist
Discoverer of The Peter Principle

 Van Nostrand Reinhold Company
New York / Cincinnati / Toronto / London / Melbourne

Howard Chapman, the artist for this book, resides in Alexandria, Virginia, and is currently the Art Director for the *Congressional Quarterly*.

Van Nostrand Reinhold Company Regional Offices:
New York Cincinnati Chicago Millbrae Dallas

Van Nostrand Reinhold Company International Offices:
London Toronto Melbourne

ISBN: 0-442-20926-6

Manufactured in the United States of America

Published by Van Nostrand Reinhold Company
450 West 33rd Street, New York, N. Y. 10001

Published simultaneously in Canada by Van Nostrand Reinhold Ltd.

15 14 13 12 11 10 9 8 7 6 5 4 3

This Book is Dedicated—

To the officials of the Agency for International Development and the Department of State who first inspired me to mumble; and

To my wife, Irene, who has mumbled with me throughout the hemisphere; to our sons, Richard Vincent and James Stanley, who tried to understand my utterances; to my parents, James B. and Una Lee, who have encouraged in all endeavors; and

To Robin Ahrold, David Allred, Mae Axton, Rex Baker, Richard Barnes, Aida Berio, Brian Beun, Robert Boger, Isabel Boger, Gene Boren, Lyle Boren, David Boren, Susan Boren, Riley Boren, Edward Brooks, John Buckley, William Bullard, Marathon Bullard, George Butts, Floyd Cash, Mike Causey, Ping Chen, Howard Chapman, Fred Cheek, Frances B.A. Cheek, Dorothy Corn, W. R. Corvin, Art Cox, John Cramer, William Crawford Sr. and Jr., Allan Cromley, Fred Dyer, Drysdales of Randolph, Ed Edstrom, Addine Erskine, Mignon Euans, Dante Fascell, Rudy Fascell, Jim Finley, Nancy Firmin, Jack Fishburne, Wade Fleetwood, William Forington, Peter Gamble, Frank Gatteri, Tom Gauger, Tom Gavin, Don and Peg Gould, Walter Graham, Jim Grazier, Michael Hamilton, Woodrow Hamilton, Ella Harllee, Harold Harriger, Charles Haydon, Harden and Weaver, Evelyn Hayes, David Hearne, H. K. Henley, Hertels of Randolph, Robert Hoving, Donald Howard, Glenn Howard, Ray Hulick, William Hunter, Ann Jenkins, Richard Jewell, Charles Johnston, Minnie Johnston, Tobias Johnston, Dee Kerns, Dixie Kilham, Frank Kimball, Grover Kincaid, Larry King, John Koval, Clyde Lamotte, Jean Lewis, Vernon Louviere, Neil V. McNeil, Mike Maloof, Dallace Marable, Larry McShane, Frank Merklein, Darcy Mesquita, Jayme Messeder, Robert Miller, John Moore, Billy Charles Newbold, Frances Newby, Wilma Ogilvie, Ed Orr, Sandra Padilla, Jim Pearson, Laurence and Irene Peter, Gertrude Phelan, Will Pirkey, Sherman Pratt, Senator Jennings Randolph, Bernard Rapoport, Buell Craig Raupe, Roberto Rendon, Forrest Rettgers, Edgar Ribas, Betty Hoyenga Richardson, Nelson Robinson, George Sánchez, Mariano Sánchez, Emery Sanford, Ben Schwartz, Ron Shafer, Roland Shipman, Robert Smith, Mariflor de Solis, Lou Nora Spiller, Marilyn Stafford, Tom Stafford, Cleve Stauffer, Steve Stephens, Danny the Stringer, Frank Taylor, Ted Tenorio, Arthur Tonsmeire Jr., Irving Tragen, Vivian Vahlberg, Jack Hood Vaughn, Art Warner, Jack Weems, Jewell Weems, Weston Weems, Ben Wells, Jeanette Westfall, Charles Wiggin, Danny Williams, Glen Wilson, Boni Wittenbrink, Congressman Jim Wright, Senator Ralph Yarborough, another Yarborough, Joseph Young, *and to all my other creditors.*

James H. Boren

Introduction

In the life of each great man, there comes at least one occasion when he must pass the test of a "finest hour"—a moment in time when man and circumstance contribute mutually to the establishment of a hero image.

Dr. James Harlan Boren's "hour" came on Tuesday, June 22, 1971, as he testified before the House Public Works Subcommittee on Investigation and Oversight. It was clear from the outset that a new leader had bubbled to the surface of the political cesspool. As Boren proceeded to expound on "dynamic inaction and constructive nonresponsiveness," he demonstrated his grasp of the bureaucratic commitment to furthering the *status quo* by recommending a new cabinet-level Department of Red Tape. This department, to coordinate paper work, would have divisions such as the Office of Over-runs Permeations and Statistics (OOPS), Governmental Linguistics Obtusity Bureau (GLOB), Computerized Lethargic Output Division (CLOD), and Management Unite for Maximized Budgetary and Legal Evaluations (MUMBLE). Is it any wonder that this man, recommending to a congressional subcommittee more red tape instead of less, was the president of the National Association of Professional Bureaucrats, bureaucratically abbreviated to NATAPROBU?

Jim Boren is the bureaucrat's bureaucrat, the incarnation of the only constant in the variable equation of the modern military-industrial-political complex. In every hierarchy in civilized society, bureaucrats hiding among piles of paper, carbon copies, and paper clips have waited for the coming of a leader. The Boren genius lies in his sensitivity to the unmet needs of this immense unorganized segment of society, the professional bureaucrats. NATAPROBU is dedicated to optimizing the *status quo* by fostering adjustive adherence to procedural abstractions and rhetorical clearances by means of promoting feasibility studies, reviews, surveys of plans, surveys of feasibility studies, and surveys of reviews. Stated nonbureaucratically, dynamic inactivism is great input that produces little output.

With his tongue in both cheeks, Jim Boren helps us to understand the saga of Rolls-Royce, Lockheed, the Pentagon, and all other escalations where expenditure is colossal and everything is recorded in some diabolical archive, but individual responsibility or achievement is minimal. As bureaucratic influence grows, the individual is under constant pressure beyond his control and he is bereft of an audible voice as rules, regulations, forms, and established guidelines limit his effectiveness.

In this book, Jim Boren describes eloquently the various functions of the bureaucrat but says little regarding the development of the bureaucracy. It therefore appears appropriate that in these introductory remarks I provide a brief case history to illustrate bureaucratic development.

Porno Press, publisher of Hard Core Books, is housed in a high-rise building with many employees of the lowest rank on the ground floor, somewhat fewer employees on the second floor, fewer still on the third, and so on up to the top where founder-president Ty Kune has his well-appointed suite of offices. Porno Press is a typical hierarchy. Employees are arranged in ranks with a system of promotion from one rank to another.

A change in obscenity legislation precipitated a sudden upswing in the sales of Hard Core Books. As orders poured in, the backlog of back orders, requisitions, and letters requesting books completely swamped the shipping department. Output decreased. Customers complained.

It was apparent that the shipping department was the major bottleneck, and Ty Kune decided to meet the challenge by increasing the staff in the shipping department. A batch of new employees was hired. Each had a college diploma proving that he had been a competent student. This qualified him for a promotion to the world of commerce, or from being unemployed to being employed. Let us call them One to Ten.

The ten recruits were assigned the rank of Mail Order Processor and given desks on the ground floor. Each man was handed a pile of orders and shown how to process them.

Two years passed. It is time for a round of promotions at Porno Press. Let us see how employees One to Ten have fared.

Messrs. One to Five, in various ways, have proven themselves incompetent as Mail Order Processors. Mr. One often forgets to record the customer's remittance. As a result, his accounts of cash receipts and orders approved do not balance. Mr. Two is careless with his rubber stamp. He often stamps a big black ORDER AP-PROVED FOR SHIPMENT right over the customer's name and address, or over the title of the book requested. This produces a stream of complaints from the Shipping Department. Mr. Three is persistently unpunctual and spends his hours pursuing the contents of Hard Core Books. Mr. Four is a poor salesman. When the book that a customer orders is not available, he simply stamps the order

OUT OF PRINT or CONFISCATED BY CUSTOMS and refunds the money. He will not take the trouble to suggest a suitable alternate title.

Mr. Five's mind is not on his job. He belongs to the Bachelors' Association for Legitimate Literature in Society (BALLS) and writes indignant letters to the FBI protesting the distribution of dirty books. In addition, he has the worst possible girl friend for a man in his position. She is an editor for a rival publisher, Passion Press, publishers of Sin Sear Books. The Porno Press management fears that if Mr. Five was promoted to a responsible position, he might betray the Porno mailing list to his girl friend. He might even reveal the names of the pseudonymous authors who write Hard Core books.

So these five are not eligible for promotion. They have reached their level of incompetence. They will remain at the lowest rank in the positions they are incompetent to fill.

Messrs. Six to Ten have worked competently in the lowest rank and are eligible for promotion to Wholesale Order Processor. They now have to deal with large orders from bookstores, military establishments, libraries, book clubs, schools, and colleges. Each of them must also supervise a few employees of lower rank.

Two more years pass. Of the five promotees, three have proven incompetent. Mr. Six cannot stand the extra responsibility, and has developed a peptic ulcer. Mr. Seven is mentally unequipped for the more complex difficult work and is too slow at making decisions. His memos to his subordinates are unintelligible. Mr. Eight does his own paper work effectively, but cannot supervise the work of his subordinates. Excellent at obeying orders, he does not know how to issue them. When he does not get his way immediately, he acts the bully. At other times he tries to be friendly but still cannot win respect.

So Six, Seven, and Eight have achieved final placement at their levels of incompetence. They are not eligible for further promotion. They will not be fired. They will simply remain at their present rank, vainly trying to do the work they cannot do.

Messrs. Nine and Ten, having shown themselves competent at this level, are promoted to the rank of Assistant Editor. They now have to deal with temperamental and difficult authors, artists, photographers, and printers. Often they have to take manuscripts and proofs home with them evenings and weekends. Each Assistant Editor is held responsible for the success or failure of the books that he has recommended, sponsored, and processed.

Three years later, Mr. Nine's social drinking has developed, under the strain of his work and worry, into alcoholism. He is often away from the office. When he comes in, he cannot concentrate on his work. He has reached his level.

Mr. Ten is successful as Assistant Editor, so is eventually promoted to Editor. He proved to be competent at that, too, and four years later became Senior Editor. In this position, however, the strain began to show and he suffered from hypertension, nervousness, and impotence. He began making irrational decisions. His doctor told him, "Slow down. Take it easy. Don't work so hard."

He slowed down. He took it easy. But he still made irrational decisions. In other words, he has become an incompetent Senior Editor and is barred from further promotion until death, retirement, or commitment to the State Home for the Bewildered rescue him from his dilemma.

All ten employees are now at their respective levels of incompetence. The increased input, the addition of Messrs. One to Ten, is now producing no increased output. As a matter of fact, Messrs. One, Two, Five, Eight, and Ten are definite liabilities and seriously impede output.

How does Ty Kune try to cope with incompetence as opportunity for expansion increases? He makes rules. He hires administrative assistants who become rule enforcers. When situations arise that are outside of existing rules, the administrators either insist that conditions be modified to conform with the rules, or they make new rules to cover the marginal condition. As the enforcement of rules and escalation of rules increase, more and more individuals are employed as rule makers and rule enforcers. Ty Kune and his department heads, managers, supervisors, and supervisory assistants are now all bureaucrats.

With the escalation of bureaucracy, Porno Press can now accommodate more incompetence. Individual initiative, creativity, and competence are no longer requisites for hierarchal status. Conformity to the established rules is now all that is required. Where this is not possible and an employee cannot even produce ritualistic conformity, the bureaucrat responds by producing more supervision, more instructions, and more red tape.

This situation, of course, cannot be blamed on any special weakness in the personnel policy or Porno Press. The same thing is happening in government, the military, education, and every organization whose members are arranged in ranks, with a system of promotion from rank to rank.

Dr. Boren has observed new departments of government that initially served some useful purpose mature into bureaucracies of ineptitude. At the lowest levels of officialdom, he has seen information officers who refuse to give out information and humorless, petty bureaucrats whose lives are devoted to ritualistic conformity to rules, regulations, and meaningless paper work. At middle management levels he has encountered the pompous status seeker pontificating about the importance and responsibility of his office while he evades real responsibility by blaming the system, his superiors, and his subordinates. He has studied the bureaucrat at the executive level and eloquently described how, through the appointment and manipulation of committees, task forces, and commissions, it is possible to delay constructive action indefinitely, and how the chief executive of a bureaucracy, by relying on studies, reports, and opinion polls, can remain a nominal leader while in reality he is the ultimate follower.

Boren has conceptualized the bureaucracy as a continually escalating, nonresponsive, self-serving, self-perpetuating organism, operated by men dedicated to self-abnegating bureaucratic behavior. It is this behavior that Boren describes in this handbook. His method is satire but his observations are accurate. He is not trying to make the world safe for bureaucracy. His battle cry "Bureaucrats of the world, unite—you have nothing to lose but your brains!" is a warning about the future, if we do not recognize the bureaucrat for what he is.

Boren's message is for everyone. Even bureaucrats are the victims of the escalation and perpetuation of the bureaucratic system. As bureaucracy advances, the *status quo* is defended long past the point where the *quo* has lost its *status*.

LAURENCE J. PETER,
Hierarchiologist,
Discoverer of The Peter Principle.

THE BUREAUCRAT'S SOLILOQUY

To clear, or not to clear: that is the question:
Whether 'tis wiser in the end to accept
The taunts and curses of an outraged people,
Or to take arms against a change of policy,
And by studying end it? To clear; to stall;
No more; and by so stalling work to end
The heartache and the thousand natural shocks
Bureaus are hier to; 'tis a prolongation
Devoutly to be wish'd. To clear; to stall;
To stall, perchance to think: Ay, there's the rub;
For in those thoughts of man what threats may come
To undermine the bureaucratic role,
Must give us pause. There's the respect
That makes calamity of public life;
For who would bear the ills that change may bring,
The drafter's prose, the precise expression,
The pangs of decisiveness, the simple form,
The insolence of people, and the loss
When finger tapping no longer reigns supreme,
When he himself might his quietus make
By resignation?—Who would action stop,
To grunt and sweat under a weary life,
But that the dread of something different,
The undiscover'd country from whose bourn
No bureaucrat returns, puzzles the will,
And makes us rather hold that which we have
Than to fly to changes that we know not of?
Thus *status quo* makes heroes of us all;
And thus the sanctity of proper channels
Avoids attack from the pale cast of thought,
And enterprises of great change and danger
With this regard their currents turn awry,
And lose the name of action.
                                    James H. Boren

Contents

PART ONE   The Communications Skills of Professional Bureaucrats

PART TWO   Academic and Corporate Thrumming

PART THREE   Career Programming for Promotion and Survival

PART FOUR   Organizational Technology of the Professional Bureaucrat

PART FIVE   Random Thoughts of a Professional Bureaucrat

WHEN
IN
DOUBT,
MUMBLE

1

The Communications Skills of Professional Bureaucrats

The Call to Inaction

THE DEDICATED BUREAUCRAT
APPEARED VERY EARLY IN MAN'S HISTORY

rise, oh ye bureaucrats of the world, and lift thy voices in inseparable but resonant tones. Go ye forth across the continents of the earth, and mumble abidingly among the people. For the dawn of the golden age of inaction is upon us, and the world will soon be ours.

Know ye that from the beginning of time, man has been engaged in a constant struggle with the forces of Nature. He has sought to moderate the changes wrought by the tides of the seas, and he has tried to reduce the effects of great variances of humidity and temperature that plague mankind in much of the world. He has fought to control the erosion of the land by leveling the flow of water and wind that accompany the changing of Nature's seasons. He has fought against the constancy of change that is at the heart of Nature's mysteries.

But the noblest of all of man's struggles are those in which dedicated bureaucrats, armed with the spirit of dynamic inaction, have fought to protect the ramparts of creative nonresponsiveness from the onslaughts of mere citizens who have demanded action in their behalf. Through the ages, valiant men and women have fought the apostles of change and have successfully preserved the sacred nature of the *status quo.* In the forefront of the battles have been the professional bureaucrats, who have insisted that change is dangerous and progress is the world's greatest mistake.

While scientists have searched for the patterns of Nature's rules of change, and while philosophers have probed for the profound meanings that may be hidden in those patterns, the professional bureaucrats have attacked with crusading zeal the institutions that have dared to seek change in the social order. While poets have been inspired by the beauty that is woven into the fabric of Nature's mysteries and composers have translated life's patterns into beautiful symponies, the professional bureaucrats have thrummed steadfastly to perfect the intricate system of inaction that may save bureaucracy from the dangers of new ideas and potential change.

The state of the bureaucratic art today permits great personal fulfillment for those persons who dedicate their lives to the principles of dynamic inaction and constructive decision avoidance. By applying the techniques of orbital dialoguing and giving free rein to policy formulation by subliminal thought processes, the professional bureaucrat can foster the mumbling artistry of the adjustive *status quo.*

The state of the art, however, can no longer be considered only the art of the state. A bureaucrat today *may* be a government employee, but he also may be a master of the multi-rhythmic art of the corporate or academic worlds. The professional bureaucrat (hereinafter also to be referred to as "probu") is, above all things, a person dedicated to the optimization of the *status quo.* The probu can devitalize ideas with deft thrusts of yesbuttisms and forthright avoidisms. Constructive interface avoidance and steadfast decision postponement are the finest products of the bureaucrat's art.

The fact that a bureaucrat can no longer be defined merely as an employee of a governmental bureau is testimony to the outstanding growth of "The Movement."[1] Today, every area of human endeavor is being influenced by the organizational patterns, orbital dialoguing techniques, and dynamic inaction that characterize the billowing bureaucracies that are rapidly settling over the earth as a great blanket of protective compatibility.

Fellow bureaucrats of the world, let us raise our eyes to the horizon and find that brilliant star of hope to guide our footsteps along that thorny path that we all must traverse before we arrive at the harbor of safety and peace. Marching forward with renewed dedication to the proposition that change is dangerous, let us fight to bring about a new world order in which *status quo* can take its proper place in the field of innovation—within established guidelines.

Let us arise and go forth in the cause of the creative *status quo.* Let us serve as recruiters and teachers of a new generation of bureaucrats. Let us move across the land and organize committees.

---

[1]What is known in Washington, D.C., as simply "The Movement" is known in other parts of the nation as "The Bureaucratic Movement" or "The BM." The term refers to the flow of bureaucracy from Washington to other parts of the nation.

2

Communicating in the Written Idiom

WITH REGARD TO YOUR RAISE, WE CANNOT ARRIVE AT AN EXPEDITED, HUMANISTIC ACCOMMODATION

(BUZZ WORD, ORGANOGRAM APPLICATION III, CODE 463)

n any well-organized bureaucracy, the *theme* of communication is less important than the *artistry* with which words, charts, and other tools of communication are used. Rhetorical artistry reigns supreme in the substantive aesthetics of the art. Bureaucratic experience reflects that junior executives or beginning bureaucrats must learn to use the qualifying abstractions that spell the difference between routine presentations and neutral masterpieces.

For example, a developing bureaucrat might write, "On the basis of the documented report of the committee, I recommend the proposal be rejected." A rank beginner might .even say, "I recommend the proposal be rejected." Such statements attest to a total lack of artistry and a failure to comprehend the principles of dynamic inactivism.

An accomplished bureaucrat would express himself with qualifying definition: "While the initial study committee has made a skillful and in-depth analysis of the alternative resource mixes as they relate to the proposal in question, the optimal functions as reflected by the committee's thematic projections would suggest a nonaffirmative response if the executive office were forced to make an immediate decision. In view of the paramount importance of the multivious aspects of the proposal, it is my recommendation that a special task force be created with the assigned responsibility of appropriately developing sound administrative options to the proposed implementation decision. Reliable and tested administrative procedures would enhance the practicality of the proposal and add to it the incremental viability factors essential for the type of creative innovation that functions within established guidelines."

As an aid to budding practitioners of the bureaucratic art, senior probus recommend three basic approaches to learning to write the language of the professional bureaucrat. The three are not exclusive but are instead complementary and integratory in nature. The three approaches are: (1) thesauric formula, (2) constructive emulation, and (3) buzz-word utilization.

The thesauric formula is an unsophisticated but effective approach to bureaucratic expression. The trainee should state in very simple terms the idea he wishes to express. The statement then should be embellished with the qualifying adjectives and adverbs that will provide interpretive flexibility. Such an approach will permit the statement to stand the test of time and policy change.

Assume, for example, that a bureaucrat wishes to state, "I doubt that it will work." By using the thesauric formula of word-phrase substitution, he could write, "It is my present view that there are serious doubts about the implementation of the plan." An additional thesauric touch might translate the sentence into: "Given my present vantage point, it would appear that there are questionable, or at best, undemonstrable elements that might negatively affect the ultimate implementation of the integrated program."

Roget's International Thesaurus is the constant companion of the professional bureaucrat; with it, a probu can master the art of opalescent communication.

The constructive emulation approach involves the *semantical echo* of outstanding models. Harmonic use of adjective and adverbial strings can be found in the works of noted corporate, academic, and governmental bureaucrats. Developing bureaucrats can learn to write with fuzzistic artistry if they will study the fine and authoritative works of professional practitioners of the art. Semantical echoes of skilled practitioners embody elements of the thesauric formula, but the harmonized stringing varies from bureaucrat to bureaucrat just as spondees may vary from poet to poet.

An official of the U. S. Department of State made a major contribution to the national archives with a treatise that included an inspiring section on "The Qualitative Quantitative Interface." The official's definition of national interests reflects a highly developed communicative skill and lends itself to constructive emulation.

We define national interests as *internally generated and outward flowing forces from within any country which bind that country in some structured way to another country.* National interests are in part physical—hence readily susceptible of quantitative evaluation (numbers of expatriate American citizens; dollars of overseas business investments; volume of foreign trade); in part psycho-social and/or historo-cultural—hence qualitative, intuitive and largely incapable of meaningful quantitative definition; *in part entirely abstract* (strategic significance of one country to another; the political stance of one country vis-a-vis a third country of mutual significance). While abstract, the latter are nevertheless entirely valid and "real" interests. They are amenable to systematic treatment and also may appropriately involve aspects of quantitative analysis. Conclusions from such analysis however, cannot be based exclusively on numerical treatment of relationships so defined.[1]

In addition to high-level policy papers, the developing probu should read as many memoranda as possible. Management memoranda provide excellent illustrations for future replication. For example, a governmental memorandum concerning "subject files" reflects fuzzistic approach to communication. "These files are organized for convenience by Manual Order subject inasmuch as most, if not all, conceivable subjects for the file are comprehended in the Manual Order system."[2]

Other resources for constructive emulation are annual reports of major corporations, proceedings of conventions of educators, orations of public officials, reports from the Pentagon, and press releases from the Department of Housing and Urban Development. Tonal infusions and contextual ineffability are characteristics of proper involutions.

Sentence structure can also be a helpful instrument in fostering middle-level communication. A senior public official, for example, described progress toward Indian self-determination in these terms: "A newly reorganized Bureau of Indian Affairs, with almost all-Indian leadership, will from now on be concentrating its resources on a program of reservation-by-reservation development, including redirection of employment assistance to strengthen reservation economies, creating local Indian Action Teams for manpower train-

[1]Redecker, John Brayton, *CASP, A Systematic Approach to Policy Planning and Analysis in Foreign Affairs,* a paper prepared for a symposium of the Military Operations Research Society, San Diego, California, November, 1969.

[2]Calhoun, Richard F., A/MP NOTICE #47, Agency for International Development, August 31, 1971. Memorandum written on United States Government Memorandum form: Optional Form No. 10, May, 1962, Edition, GSA (41 CFR) 101-11.6.

ing, and increased contracting of education and other functions to Indian communities."[3]

The use of acronyms, or what is also known as "government initials," is the helpful instrument for probus. Nonpractitioners of the bureaucratic art, however, sometimes despair at what they consider to be a difficult language. Congressman Jim Wright, for example, put his concern in poetic form. He wrote:

> We have bureaus, departments and boards of review,
> And various assortments of agencies who
>
> Write guidelines to restrict
> And draw charts to depict
> The wandering maze that we try to go through.
>
> But it boggles the mind to seek comprehension
> As witnesses speak in the fourth dimension,
> And glibly refer with such effortless ease
> To each thought and concept in governmentese.
>
> There is AASHO and ARBA and T-E-U
> And TOPICS and ARC and the C-E-Q;
> There is AWP and AHFWP and A-S-A-P
> And all are involved with the DOT.
>
> P-W and EDA have an O-E-D-P
> That sometimes runs afoul of R-C&D,
> But if SODA and FCEDD seem confusing to you
> They're quite simply explained by a man named Gigoux.
>
> The O-E-P tries to get help quick
> To disaster-hit towns that are stricken and sick,
> But the O-E-P works through C of E,
> S-B-A, H-E-W, and H-U-D,
> Its own F-C-O and the D-O-T—
> And how all this gets done is a mystery to me.
>
> There is NEPA and EPA and F-A-R,
> And "Impact Statements" from near and far;
> There is the P-B-S of the G-S-A
> For which one Bob Kunzig has overall say;
> But follow the thread and you'll finally see
> That all of it's run by the O-M-B.
>
> And though you might think there's no man alive
> Who understands Circular A-95,
> I am told that some do

[3]White House Press Release. State of the Union Message of President Nixon Presented to the Members of the Second Session of the 92nd Congress, January 20, 1972.

And though they be few
They are less naive than I, or you
Who are trying to prune this red tape tree
With the very dull sword of Don Quixote—
And I sometimes think how foolish are we.[4]

Though Congressman Wright has failed to grasp the beauty of dynamic inaction, his words nevertheless pay tribute to an important part of the probu's communication system.

An official of the Department of Housing and Urban Development was asked the question, "Do you feel that 'gobbledygook' is a problem in the Federal Government?" He replied:

HUD administers some 70 plus programs, most of which are authorized by a specific piece of legislation. In our shorthand, the programs are referred to by the title number or section number of the authorizing legislation, and we tend to carry the shorthand into the *outside world*. We habitually refer to the program of subsidized home ownership, for example, as the "235" program (Section 235, National Housing Act). Indeed, this usage has gained considerable currency in the public domain.[5]

The HUD official's response to the potential critic reflected dedicated adherence to bureaucratic patterns of communication. Though the *inside world* must be protected by procedures and channels from the *outside world,* probus in all domains should seek to expand the use of bureaucratic language.

In addition to writing in acronyms, bureaucrats should use the constructive emulation approach to improve their writing skills in order to appropriately orchestrate the adjustive interpretation patterns of the communicative plane. For example, informed sources in Washington report that even columnist Jenkin Lloyd Jones had difficulty translating an inter-office memo from the Department of the Interior. The memo read: "The appropriate concepts of cost and gain depend upon the level of optimization, and the alternative policies that are admissible. This appropriate level of optimization

---

[4]*Hearings on Red Tape,* The Investigations and Oversight Subcommittee of the Public Works Committee, House of Representatives, June, 1971. Poem of Congressman Jim Wright.

[5]Haught, Robert L., *The Language of Government,* an unpublished paper, The University of Oklahoma, August 20, 1971. A Department of Defense official indicated to Mr. Haught that some disparity exists in the communicative skills of military and civilian employees of the department. He said, "Military officers are taught to write clearly. Most civilian officials of the Defense Department have at least adequate ability for understandable self-expression."

and the alternatives that should be compared depend in part on the search for a suitable criterion."[6]

Buzz words are perhaps the most useful of all tools for enabling developing bureaucrats to immediately express thoughts in acceptable bureaucratic terms.[7] While the buzz words were developed with sections stressing academic, corporate, and governmental harmonics, the interdisciplinary applications are compatible. Note Organogram One A/Alpha.

ORGANOGRAM ONE A/ALPHA
For bureaucratic buzz phrases, think of a three-digit number. Select the corresponding word from each column, and you will be able to write or speak with "orchestrated rhetorical integrity." (That is 899 of General Application I!)

GENERAL APPLICATION 0   (Interpretive educatory harmonics)

0. restructured	0. threshold	0. pattern
1. nondirective	1. motivational	1. dynamics
2. definitive	2. developmental	2. principles
3. steadfast	3. historo-cultural	3. guidance
4. in-service	4. disciplinary	4. relationship
5. individualized	5. educational	5. norm
6. achieved	6. supervisory	6. counseling
7. implied	7. enrichment	7. accreditation
8. regressive	8. parental	8. testing
9. unique	9. resource-intensive	9. rate

GENERAL APPLICATION 00   (Interpretive commercial harmonics)

0. subordinated	0. multiphasic	0. debenture
1. computerized	1. executive	1. dividends
2. encumbered	2. precommital	2. parameter
3. projected	3. regulatory	3. revenues
4. additive	4. transmittal	4. preclusion
5. moderated	5. fractional	5. conglomerate
6. modified	6. liability	6. imputation
7. restructured	7. residual	7. sector
8. recapitalized	8. investment	8. issue
9. quantitized	9. flexible	9. subsidiary

[6]Among the informed sources in Washington, Mr. Haught, as a key member of the staff of Senator Henry Bellmon, has orbitally dialogued on the "language of government" and has devoted much study to the semantical interfacing of polibus (political bureaucrats) on Capitol Hill.

[7]The history of buzz-word development is somewhat enbrangled, but Philip Broughton of the United States Public Health Service is credited with the first major United States publication of a basic 30-word system. Mr. Broughton was given special recognition for his buzz-word contributions when the National Association of Professional Bureaucrats presented him with a NATAPROBU Distinguished Service Award at the Bureaucrats Ball of 1967, held at the Mosby Inn, Fairfax, Virginia, on June 28, 1968. Mr. Broughton indicated that his research on the origination of the buzz-word systemization led him to an unidentifiable officer in the Royal Canadian Air Force.

TABLE *(continued)*

GENERAL APPLICATION I   (Academic programming with governmental inputs)

0. systematic	0. evidential	0. avoidance
1. interfaced	1. hypothetical	1. synthesis
2. programized	2. motivational	2. survey
3. multi-disciplinary	3. adjustive	3. methodology
4. conceptualized	4. institutional	4. analysis
5. low key	5. confrontational	5. framework
6. disadvantaged	6. empirical	6. procedures
7. departmentalized	7. professional	7. reaction
8. orchestrated	8. manpower	8. determinism
9. maximized	9. rhetorical	9. integrity

GENERAL APPLICATION II   (Emphasis on corporate thrumming)

0. orchestrated	0. minimal	0. dialogue
1. undermanaged	1. analytical	1. allocation
2. computerized	2. coordination	2. feasibility
3. incrementalized	3. procurement	3. guidelines
4. applied	4. tactical	4. infrastructure
5. unitized	5. orbital	5. breakthrough
6. finalized	6. financial	6. subsidiary
7. innovative	7. technological	7. implementation
8. optimized	8. interpretive	8. input
9. encumbered	9. variable	9. thrust

GENERAL APPLICATION III   (Interdisciplinary dialogues)

0. preferential	0. revisionary	0. proliferation
1. reoriented	1. duplicate	1. instrumentation
2. upgraded	2. compatible	2. sovereignty
3. restructured	3. tripartite	3. accommodation
4. expedited	4. auditing	4. repression
5. enhanced	5. environmental	5. development
6. progressive	6. humanistic	6. incompatibility
7. interdepartmental	7. categorical	7. consultancy
8. militant	8. discrete	8. hardware
9. enriched	9. sophisticated	9. certification

GENERAL APPLICATION IV   (Revelant semantical infusions)

0. essential	0. mobile	0. options
1. functional	1. bilateral	1. dissent
2. horizontal	2. management	2. nonresponsiveness
3. authorized	3. oratorical	3. policies
4. professional	4. systematic	4. negotiations
5. rigid	5. logistical	5. leadership
6. uncertain	6. institutional	6. agencies
7. inconstant	7. qualitative	7. obligations
8. prescribed	8. tertiary	8. fluctuations
9. official	9. concise	9. regulations

GENERAL APPLICATION V   (Ponderable communicative projections)

0. counterpart	0. executive	0. controversy
1. calculated	1. empirical	1. research
2. comparative	2. plausible	2. rejoinder
3. strategic	3. philosophical	3. rationale
4. cumulative	4. abstract	4. requirements
5. supportable	5. alternative	5. criteria

TABLE *(continued)*

6. harmonized	6. cautious	6. deliberations
7. total	7. optional	7. rejection
8. exhaustive	8. viable	8. advocacy
9. substantive	9. academic	9. documentation

GENERAL APPLICATION VI   (Rhetorical simulations/ecumenical)

0. qualified	0. deliberative	0. conference
1. functional	1. collaborative	1. strategist
2. technical	2. parliamentary	2. portfolio
3. consummate	3. corporate	3. practitioner
4. contrived	4. procedural	4. proficiency
5. aggressive	5. operational	5. capability
6. collateral	6. crisis-oriented	6. involvement
7. correlated	7. rotating	7. tactician
8. unauthorized	8. administrative	8. requisition
9. contradictory	9. authoritative	9. spectrum

GENERAL APPLICATION VII   (Cohesive confrontational avoidance)

0. accredited	0. responsive	0. studies
1. adapted	1. relevant	1. performance
2. documented	2. counterpart	2. regulations
3. qualitative	3. domestic	3. fluctuations
4. corrective	4. management	4. approximations
5. institutionalized	5. corporate	5. disparity
6. harmonized	6. anticipatory	6. linkage
7. consistent	7. fiscal	7. stipulations
8. evaluated	8. budgetary	8. concurrence
9. meaningful	9. reciprocal	9. diplomacy

GENERAL APPLICATION VIII   (Articulated prolusions)

0. summarized	0. informational	0. stabilization
1. maximum	1. ethical	1. contingency
2. perceptive	2. concurrent	2. validity
3. systematized	3. logistical	3. committees
4. mobilized	4. multilateral	4. structure
5. tabulated	5. supervisory	5. uniqueness
6. proficient	6. counterproductive	6. liquidity
7. vertical	7. definitive	7. instrumentalities
8. comprehensive	8. variable	8. placement
9. adjustive	9. manpower	9. endeavors

Use of the buzz words enables a beginning bureaucrat to write with the apparent skill of the experienced bureaucrat. For example, the following message can be proluded with the use of the number 979:

The VI-004 with which the VI-115 can effect an overall VI-756 depends, in part, on the VI-683 of the VI-249. Of course, if the VII-250 conflict with the VII-566, it may be advisable to utilize the VII-384 as a means of harmonizing the VIII-847.

Translated by the buzz-word chart, this becomes:

The unique enrichment rate at which the quantitized residual subsidiary can effect an overall unitized executive balance depends, in part, on the maximized professional integrity of the encumbered technological thrust. Of course, if the enriched categorical certification of the official qualitative regulations conflict with the substantive optional documentation, it may be advisable to utilize the contradictory rotating spectrum as a means of harmonizing the meaningful fiscal diplomacy.

In addition to employing the buzz words with a single three-digit number in different applicatory sections, a combination of numbers may be applied within single or multiple sections. For example, if the young corporate bureaucrat wishes to make a business forecast, he might write:

The 00-111 appears to be within the 00-200 of the 00-883. If the 00-091 continue toward the 00-339 for the 00-925, it is indicative of a 00-642. Prudent management and appropriate action will result in a 00-039 program.

Diligent practice can bring the bureaucratic practitioner to the 00-671 within I-086 in a minimum of time!

To master the techniques of bureaucratic communication, the probu should practice the three basic approaches at every opportunity. The linguistic involutions can inspire citizens to function with total dedication to the principles of dynamic inaction. Constant practice is the key to such semantical profundication.

It is important, therefore, that bureaucrats who wish to communicate their concepts of nonresponsiveness to others should practice their translation skills at every opportunity. When reading the morning paper, for example, the bureaucrat can practice translating the headlines into professional terminology; or, when reading a memorandum from a bureaucratic colleague, he can mentally rephrase it to conform to higher professional standards. Even writing the grocery list for shopping purposes can provide an opportunity to practice semantical translations. Instead of writing "potatoes" on the grocery shopping list, for example, the bureaucrat can note, "If appropriately compatible to the taste spectrum as relates to the optimal state of maturity, one sack of potatoes." Men and women who devote time and effort to expressing thoughts in professional terms will rise in their institutional hierarchy. They will also find great satisfaction in attaining the status of a recognized profundicator.

To write a message with the poetic profundity of the professional bureaucrat is to encourage the implementation of dynamic inaction. 'Tis communicative enrichment devoutly to be wished.

Mumbling with Professional Eloquence

THE MUMBLER MUST PROJECT
UTMOST SINCERITY!

he skills involved in developing professional fluency are closely intertwined with those of the successful ponderer and competent writer. The spoken word, however, lends itself to constructive opacity that can buy important time for the bureaucrat to assess carefully the parameters of the conference. When he is in doubt about either the issues being discussed or the policy predisposition of his superiors, the bureaucrat may articulately mumble his neutral thoughts.

ARTICULATE MUMBLING

Articulate mumbling should not be viewed with disdain or treated in jest; it is an effective tool that can serve both the professional and the developing bureaucrat equally well. A careful study of artistic mumblers reveals that there are basically two approaches to this form of communication. They are: (1) linear and (2) vertical. The approach or classification utilized by practitioners appears to be a function primarily of personal taste.[1]

[1]NATAPROBU-sponsored research into the matter is still in process, but there is some evidence that years of service may influence the choice between linear and vertical mumbling. With maturation, the bureaucrat tends to make greater use of the vertical approach, but additional empirical data will need to be collected and evaluated before a definitive statement can be made. The maturation element as it relates to the linear-vertical choice would be the subject of an interesting and constructive Ph.D. dissertation.

Linear mumbling is defined as unmodified transposition of flexible sounds. It is characterized more by tones than words. Occasional words, with linking prepositions and articles, may emerge from the tonal base of the speaker. The intelligibility should be blended with the nonverbal skills of the ponderer in such a manner as to project an impression of total knowledgeability.

Though experienced bureaucrats in Washington look to the Pentagon, the State Department, and the Department of Housing and Urban Development as the triumverate of mumblistic artistry, the White House is rapidly emerging as a source of inspiration for students of mumbling. Dr. Henry Kissinger, for example, responded with adjustive forthrightness when asked by a newsman about the Presidential trip to Peking. He was asked, "How much progress was there made in advancing the ball? How much further did we go this time than in your original talks with Premier Chou?"[2]

Dr. Kissinger replied: "The character of the discussions inevitably is entirely different when the President of the United States talks than when an assistant talks who cannot make any definite statement. The basic objective of this trip was to set in motion a train of events and an evolution in the policy of our two countries which both sides recognized would be slow at first and present many difficulties and in which a great deal depended on the assessment by each side of the understanding by the other of what was involved in this process and of the assessment by each side of the reliability of the other in being able to pursue this for the amount of time necessary to see it prevail. In this sense it almost had to be conducted by the heads of the two Governments and in this sense I would say that in the depth and seriousness of the discussions it went obviously beyond what had been discussed in my visits and beyond our expectations."[3]

For successful linear or vertical mumbling, the bureaucrat must adhere to the cardinal rule for all mumblers: THE MUMBLER MUST PROJECT UTMOST SINCERITY!

Vertical mumbling is marked by tonal intelligibility with minor overtones of translocation of syllables. Stringing words in quantitative extension is the method. It is the apparent integrity of clarity, however, that gives a sense of primacy to the utterances of the vertical mumbler. While the Pentagon and the State Department Building serve as the twin residences of outstanding vertical mum-

---

[2]*New York Times,* February 28, 1972.
[3]*Loc. cit.*

blers, educators have made their contribution to the art on a much broader geographical basis.[4]

An academic mumbler of the vertical category might say, for example, "Without wishing to restructure a delphitic projection apart from experimentation in the cross-impact matrix methodology, one should stand ready to adjust one's differentiated and totally interrelated concepts of the environment until the opinion convergence can be harmonized with the various self-structures." Integrity, bureaucratic clarity, and moderate verticality! Vertical mumbling is greatly enhanced by deep voice projection of roundly sounded vowels. The body language of the accomplished ponderer can be added to appropriate pauses in intonations to lift vertical mumbling to its highest level of perfection.

BUZZING TO SUCCESS

Tentative reviews of preliminary surveys of ongoing studies indicate that artisans in vertical mumbling tend to have an excellent working knowledge of *Roget's Thesaurus.* Buzz words can serve the beginning bureaucrat as an excellent *supplementary resource* should he determine that it is the vertical path that he wishes to pursue. Note Organogram One A/Alpha, pages 12-14.

Interwoven with the fabric of mumbling are the single-syllable words that bureaucrats may use to indicate that they are up-to-date on the casual side of communication.

> The *casual* bureaucrat should—
> *Phase out* but never kill; and *opt* but never choose.
> *Sign off* but never clear; *fall back* but never lose.
> *Draft up* but never write; *staff out* but never plan.
> *Gear up* but never start; *preclude* but never ban.

Or, if the bureaucrat wishes to move up the ladder toward the multisyllables of conversational professionalism, he may use phonic verb forms that are slightly more formal in the communication pattern.

[4]The Department of Housing and Urban Development is noted as the citadel of linear mumbling.

The formal bureaucrat should—
Implement, finalize, thrust, and embue,
Interface, maximize, meet, and review,
Orchestrate, optimize, test, and compute,
Dialogue, quantitize, rate, and refute.

MARATHON MUMBLING

The skill of marathon mumbling is one that requires hours of uninterupted practice and total devotion to conversational ineffability. Marathon mumbling involves harmonizing a series of word strings that possess qualities for deep intonation and sonic projection. Nothing can be more distasteful than to be in the presence of an amateur marathon mumbler.[5] Therefore, it behooves the dedicated learner to practice diligently in the privacy of his home or car until he has gained full command of marathon word strings.

Regardless of which mumblistic approach, however, the bureaucrat may seek as his spoken art form, there are certain skill factors common to both that, when mastered, can add to the effective dialoguing of the practitioner. These are closely interwoven with the techniques of the prodigious ponderer. Variations in modular volubility, for example, can be combined with inflectionary adjustments and facial expressions to indicate sincerity and authority.

Particularly important to mumblistic success is eye contact with the person or persons to whom the mumbling is being directed.[6] Eye contact and facial expressions that reflect knowledgeability and sincerity are the essential companions of successful linear mumbling. While knowledgeability is important, it is the projection of sincerity, however, that is the key to ineffable communication within the infrastructural patterns of mumbling.

The results of extensive research indicate that one of the most

---

[5]Accomplished marathon mumblers are few, but the number striving to perfect the skill are many. You, the reader, may become more aware of potential marathon mumblers if you will observe closely the single drivers of automobiles. When you have stopped for a traffic signal, look at the other drivers about you. It is quite probable that one day's observation will reveal at least one fellow bureaucrat proceeding through his practice steps. When you see one give him a warm smile and an encouraging gesture, for art should be encouraged for art's sake if for no other reason!
[6]The use of the suffix "istic" is used to denote purposeful planning. Thus, *mumblistic* indicates planned mumbling. *Putteristic* indicates planned, puttering, and *fuzzistic* indicates programmed fuzziness.

beautiful renditions of orchestrated mumbling ever recorded was an evening performance of the Jefferson Literary and Debating Society at the University of Virginia on February 11, 1972. From bass to soprano, from pianissimo to fortissimo, the mumblistic intonations and metarsic beats filled historic Jefferson Hall. Meeting at 7:29 P.M. every Friday since the date of its founding in 1825, the Jefferson Literary and Debating Society has devoted almost countless manhours to practicing the mumbling art.

The strong sentiment for mumbling is sensed, for example, when the secretary of the society reads the minutes of the previous meeting. The minutes are read in the mumblistic terms of total verticality, and the members of the society punctuate the minutes with infusions of linear mumbling. When the speaker for the evening of February 11, 1972, uttered his first words, he was met with rhythmic applause. As he progressed in his speech, the applause was accompanied by a rhythmic beat of feet against the oak floor of the hall. Finally, as the speaker moved to higher levels of mumbling, the members of the society mixed the applause and the beat of feet with a rising crescendo of linear mumbling.

Mass mumbling can be beautiful, and students at the University of Virginia have shown the way.

It is incumbent upon the bureaucrat, however, to master the art in order that he can not only be a participant in mass mumbling but also can one day *lead* the mumbling exercise. To develop full professionalism in mumblistic projections, the bureaucrat must learn to combine the skills of the ponderer and the mumbler in a true symphony of sound and motion.

When he cannot understand a question posed to him, or when he does not know the answer to a question that he *can* understand, the practitioner of the bureaucratic art can preserve both his dignity and his status by carefully composed mumblistic utterances.

When in doubt, mumble!

The Artistry
of Pondering

chapman

DEVELOPING PONDERERS SHOULD
PRACTICE DAILY BEFORE A MIRROR

hen a corporate employee rises to the vice presidency of his company, he has achieved the level of the prestigious ponderer who may preside but need not decide, who may delegate but need not activate, and who may review but need not do.

When a public servant rises to division chief or bureau director, he has achieved the level of the prodigious ponderer who may scrutinize but need not finalize, who may systematize but need not organize, and who may articulate but need not state.

When a teacher rises to the level of department head, principal, or dean, he has achieved the level of the pontifical ponderer who may administrate but need not illuminate, who may preach but need not teach, and who may delegate but need not educate.[1]

DIFFUSE RESPONSIBILITY

The bureaucrat in charge need not necessarily accept the risks of leadership. By diffusing responsibility through broadening his colleagues' participation in decision-making, he can optimize the *status quo* with a minimum of risk to his position.

[1]While some would equate the role of the successful ponderer to embodiment of The Peter Principle (". . . . in a hierarchy every employee tends to rise to his level of incompetence."), there are others who would steadfastly contend that the artistry of pondering reflects professional excellence, orbital eloquence, and adjustive communion. An approach to balance is the interpretive position of other students of bureaucracy.

He can preside over well-structured staff meetings, and he can appoint and coordinate the collaborative efforts of study committees, *ad hoc* committees, blue-ribbon commissions, and special task forces. He can assume the role of the prodigious ponderer and use noncommittal language forms to indicate great concern, deep meditation, and total authority.

The budding bureaucrat should study the body language of the more experienced practitioners. When the bureaucrat is asked a question about a matter on which he either knows nothing or wishes to avoid taking a position, he may use a wide variety of noncommittal techniques.

LESSONS IN PONDERING

The bureaucrat may furrow his brow while gazing intently at some imaginary heavenly body in a far corner of the room. He may slowly pucker his lips or count the number of his molars with his tongue, or he may thoughtfully stroke his chin while reclining in his chair. He may choose to softly tap his fingers on the desk or perhaps to stroke his second chin with his thumb and index fingers.

If the bureaucrat is a pipe smoker, he has a special advantage, because the image of the pipe smoker includes the inherent elements of solid character and great wisdom. Not only may the pipe smoker slowly exhale the aromatic smoke in tiny patterns of motivational gray but also he may pensively pause to refill the pipe or tap the ashes. In certain instances of great stress, he may even carefully disassemble the pipe to give it a thorough expurgation with a pipe cleaner. And he may squint his eyes and continue to furrow his brow.

The first words that a professional bureaucrat may utter at a conference may be accented by shrugging the shoulders, lifting and dropping a hand (palm upward), and popping the tongue as an added first syllable of the first word. "(*Pop*) Very good question," he may say. Then steadily looking directly into the eyes of the questioner or the most troublesome person in the meeting, the bureaucrat in charge may ask, "What is your recommendation?" Thoughtfulness proven and authority established.[2]

[2]Dr. Glen P. Wilson, psychologist and space authority, has studied the communicative impact of steady eye-to-eye contact in the bureaucratic parry, stud-and-draw poker, and jujitsu. Though his work is unpublished, he discourses regularly in the intellectual oases of Capitol Hill in Washington, and his study has contributed to the advancement of the state of the art.

Close observation of experienced bureaucrats will reveal to the trainee a skillful use of intonation in making appropriate utterances. Pitch of voice is a natural and effective companion to such body language as rolling the eyes, raising a brow, or slightly nodding the head. The tones produced may or may not be intelligible but vocal projections can emphasize a subliminal expression of doubt, concern, and neutral pondering. Inseparable but resonant tones can cast an aura of rhetorical integrity and confident authority.

PRACTICE, THE KEY TO THE ARTISTRY OF PONDERING

It is recommended that the developing bureaucrat practice daily before a mirror the wide range of skills of the successful ponderer. (See practice sheet Organogram Number Two B/Beta.) One need not be reluctant to practice before a mirror for thirty minutes each day, because progress on the institutional promotion ladder comes only to those who take pride in their profession and perfect the dexterity with which they can exude nondirective competence to their superiors.

When a trainee observes a successful ponderer, he may rest assured that the latter's success resulted from many cumulative hours spent practicing before a mirror acquiring the noninterpretive skills.

If the concert pianist can practice hours each day to share musical artistry with an appreciative audience, surely the dedicated bureaucrat can strive to enfold the art form of the masters through daily practice. In this manner he can better prepare himself for that day when he may be called upon to chair a meeting or orchestrate an entire bureau or department in a symphony of noncommittal expressions.

The bureaucrat need not act; he need not commit; he need not pursue; he need not retreat. When in charge, he need only ponder!

PONDERER'S PRACTICE SHEET

(ORGANOGRAM TWO B/BETA)

By daily practice before a mirror, the developing bureaucrat can acquire the wide range of skills of the prodigious ponderer. The successful ponderer must project total sincerity and sympathetic authority, and he should be able to articulate in the noncommital and unquotable idiom of bureaucratic gestures.

a. With brow lifted, eyes downward, mouth tightly closed inwardly, slowly straighten paper clip.

b. Hands clasped behind head, lower lip over upper lip, gaze directly overhead.

c. With mouth closed, expand each cheek alternately with intermittent puffs of air.

d. Thumb based at temple, rub brow with one to four index fingers.

e. Stroke chin with thumb and first two index fingers.

f. Head downward, lightly grasp top of head with one hand with all digits of hand (similar to grasping a cantaloupe), lightly massage scalp.

g. Lips pursed; one arm folded across chest; other elbow on hand; thumb under chin; gaze at light fixture. (May be varied if practitioner uses a swivel chair; swivel chair in thirty-degree arc— or swivel and gaze out window).

h. Thumb at base of cheek, hand over mouth, eyes upward or downward.

i. If at a desk, chin resting in one hand, tapping fingers on desk with other hand. If not at desk, right hand scratching left ear (alternately, arm in front of face or back of head).

j. With thumb and one of first two index fingers at opposite points of eyes, place elbow at chest or on desk.

k. Massage back of neck with one hand.

l. If a pipe smoker, carefully remove ashes from pipe, disassemble and clean pipe with pipe cleaner. May be accompanied by fleeting interludes of expressions p, q, r, and u. If not a pipe smoker, flip thumb (series of flips) over biting edge of upper front teeth.

m. If a pipe smoker, mouth tightly closed with lips inward, slowly light pipe; if not a pipe smoker, slowly roll pencil between thumb and index fingers of each hand.

a.

b.

c.

d.

e.

f.

g.

h.

I.

j.

k.

l.

m.

N.E.W.S. Photo-News

n. o. p.

q. r. s.

t. u. v.

w. x. y. z.

n. If at a desk, elbow on desk, forehead in hand, intermittent tapping of fingers on desk with other hand. If not at desk, gaze upward, lightly tap end of pencil or pen on pursed lips.

o. Combine expression p or q with slow doodling on note pad. (In conference sessions around a small desk, use Boren's Conceptual Doodling Technique.)

p. Lower lip over upper lip.

q. Upper teeth over lower lip.

r. Gaze at far corner, squinting one eye.

s. Head upward, eyes downward, pull at lobe of one ear.

t. With thumb at temple, lightly tap fingers on forehead.

u. Gaze at far corner of room (ceiling level).

v. With eyes fixed on some nearby object, lightly scratch head.

w. If a pipe smoker, carefully study ashes in pipe, slowly tamp ashes. If not a pipe smoker, lightly tap forehead with knuckles of clinched right hand.

x. Turn head to one side, gaze at floor.

y. With thumb and second index finger, smooth eyebrows in an inward to outward stroke beginning at point between the eyebrows.

z. With thumb under one jaw, stroke second chin with index fingers.

How to Present
a Paper

INTIMACY WITH THE AUDIENCE
CAN BE MIXED WITH SINCERITY

A probu should know more about his audience than his subject when he is presenting a paper to a learned society, a management meeting, or an interagency session. He should know, for example, how many executives will be present and how many will be accompanied by their own wives. Will the audience include board members, editors of scholarly journals, news writers, and talent scouts for other organizations? Careful analysis of the audience is important to the probu, because it will enable him to project his present and future worth to people who may play a role in his future advancement.

He should include some elements that will be pleasing to his present employer and to the key person responsible for the invitation to be on the program. He should also interlace his own future-related targets into the paper in such a way as to hit a responsive chord with the talent scouts that might hear the presentation.

Preparation of a paper is also an excellent time to use the thesauric and conservative emulation approaches in writing the first draft of the paper. The buzz words of the vertical mumbler can also be used to fill the conceptual voids that give bureaucratic credibility to the paper. The paper should be designed primarily for platform performance and only secondarily for the content.

While the probu is developing the first draft, he should seek the advice of senior probus and organizational kingpins.

PREPARING THE PAPER

Assume, for example, that the probu has been asked to give a paper on the utilization of petrified bat guano on potted palms and flowering plants. If the probu's company president considers himself an authority on bat guano and if he favors the rapid expansion of the PBG industry, the probu would be wise to include a few words in the paper that would indicate some accord with his company's leader.

If the probu was invited to present the paper by the president of an important national association, and if the association president fears that the scrape-mining of PBG will be an ecological threat, the probu should include a few words in the paper that could be interpreted as concern about the ecological implications of PBG mining. The mark of the truly professional bureaucrat is skillful use of position-avoidance techniques. By walking the line between the two positions, the probu can maintain a favorable rapport with opposing groups.

If, on the other hand, the suggestions from the probu's superior are totally out of line and therefore unusable, the probu should carefully weave into the paper a few of the superior's pet phrases or words. As the probu's superior listens to the presentation, the gestalt or "Aha, I see it now" phenomenon will come into play, and he will psychologically fill the gaps so as to recognize his contribution to the probu's paper. The other listeners will not understand, but that doesn't really matter, anyway. The presentation of papers serves as a platform for people, not messages.

When the probu strides to the speaker's stand, he should do so with a facial expression that broadcasts that he has something to say and welcomes the opportunity to say it. From the stand, the probu should survey the people in the room and make as much eye-to-eye contact as possible. This he should do before he utters the first resonant tone.

If the probu is disturbed by eye-to-eye contact, he should gaze at the forehead of those within forehead range. Such a sweep of the audience will help gain the attention of potential listeners, and will reflect the probu's self-confidence. Self-confidence and resonant tones are associated in the minds of the audience with expertise.

DELIVERY PREPARATION

Many beginning bureaucrats devote too much time to developing the substance of their messages and insufficient time to the more important factors of resonant tonal projections, rhetorical integrity, and body language. The probu should disregard the possible contradictions that annoying purists might find in his paper, and should concentrate on projecting his utterances with tones and volubility that indicate both authority and sincerity. If the probu's voice is normally weak, he should muster all volume and depth of tone possible for the first two or three sentences of his paper.

Intimacy with the audience can be woven into the fabric of sincerity by use of eyeglasses. The accomplished bureaucratic orator often interrupts his pattern of presentation by leaning forward over the speaker's lectern, removing his glasses, and speaking in what appears to be an offhand manner.

Depending on the length of the paper being presented, the glasses-off technique should be utilized by the probu only three or four times in a single presentation. If the probu does not need glasses, he can buy an inexpensive pair with nonmagnifying lenses at a variety store; he should not purchase the style with gold frames but with horn rims.

The projection of intimacy and sincerity can also be strengthened if the probu removes the glasses and places them in his breast pocket or eyeglass case during the final minutes of the presentation. This also tends to encourage the audience to prepare for appropriate applause, because it telegraphs the fact that the end of the paper is at hand.

Successful paper presenters never end the paper without clear indication that they are approaching the end. If it is not possible to transmit the message in an unobtrusive manner, the probu should use the "In conclusion. . ." phrase. Though this is not desirable, it is better than completing the paper abruptly and with no applause.

WATCH YOUR ENDINGS

Many bureaucrats inexperienced in the presentation of papers make the mistake of simply stating what they have to say and returning to their seats. This is a tragic error. Audiences deserve more consideration from readers and speakers, and should be given adequate warning of the approaching end of a paper. In this manner, the listeners can more comfortably fulfill their role as an audience, and they can indicate not only that they have been following the presentation but also that they understand it.

When the probu has completed his paper, he can announce that, in the interest of time, he will make himself available at some predetermined location and time for the purpose of answering questions. This gains the appreciation of the chairman of the proceedings, who is always concerned with "running on schedule." The people in the audience will be appreciative, too, because they will have been sitting long enough. Coffee drinkers may be even more grateful. More important, however, is that such a move heads off those other aspiring probus who—not given the opportunity to present a paper—are eager to persistently pursue some involved question, thus enabling them to raise their heads above the nest in search of some nurturing recognition. These are known as the "head raisers" and they are always present at professional conferences.

MODEL-PAPER GUIDELINES

The following illustration is presented as a guideline for paper development for those probus embarking on their first venture in an important field of bureaucratic endeavor. The opening and closing remarks can be adapted easily to almost any problem or opportunity to be the subject of a paper. The paragraphs between the opening and the closing can be adjusted according to the length suggested by the conference leaders. Statistical material makes an excellent filler. The keystone of a good paper lies not in its length or substance but in the structure of words that can permit maximum tonal projection of authority, sincerity, and concern.

> Illustrative Elements of a Paper on the
> Subject of "Utilization of Petrified Bat
> Guano on Potted Palms and Flowering Plants"

Mr. Chairman, President _____, Mayor _____, Reverend Clergy, Distinguished Guests, Ladies and Gentlemen:
It is indeed a great pleasure to once again be in the beautiful city of _____, which has a world-wide reputation for its progressive approach to urban problems in these trying times. The construction of a Little League baseball diamond, the replacement of the two diving boards at the community swimming pool, and the appointment of three study committees to study the history of _____ County demonstrate that this is a progressive city with dynamic leadership. Its great spirit is matched only by the warmth of its hospitality. So, it is indeed a great pleasure to be with you tonight to discuss with you one of the most controversial developments in the potted-plants field today.
Never before in recorded history has so much attention been drawn to the multiphasic uses of petrified bat guano. There are

those who refer to the development as an exciting new use of a natural time-release nutrient for potted palms and flowering plants. They hail it as being in keeping with the environmental thrust of organic feeding of man, animal, and plant.

There are others, however, who view the scrape-mining of petrified bat guano as an ecological threat. The removal of petrified bat guano, also known as PBG, from the limestone and hard-rock caverns may so change the cavern floor that surrounding stalagmites might be adversely affected by the altered drip-flow from the stalactites.

Now, ladies and gentlemen, there is balancing wisdom in both positions. But before detailing the results of my utilization research, we should look at the matter in proper perspective. The study of petrified bat guano can be traced to a humble but curious farmer in the hills of. . . .

(With this introduction, the probu should use the NATAPROBU Buzz Words, the constructive emulation approach, and adjustive qualifiers to build the body of the paper. The choice of words and phrases should be made with primary attention being given to the tonal projections that can reflect: (1) authority, (2) sincerity of purpose, and (3) respect for professional colleagues at the head table and in the audience. At the appropriate point in the paper, the probu may phase out the buzz words and move to the concluding remarks.)

In conclusion, ladies and gentlemen, let us come to the full realization that problems are really opportunities. If we can join forces to give petrified bat guano a small and carefully developed role in the future expansion in the potted-palm and flowering-plant industry, we can provide full-scale opportunity for in-depth study of maximized programmation of natural nutrients. This should be done, however, with cautiously bold consideration of the long-range effects that scrape-mining of PBG will have on ecological harmonics. With this in mind, therefore, I recommend that there be formed a blue-ribbon commission of ecologists and industrialists for the purpose of developing rules and regulations for the sound utilization of PBG within the ecological guidelines that can contribute to the development of the new industry. It is in this spirit of progressive compromise that we can take the best from the past for the best in the future.

Mr. Chairman, if there should be some questions on my paper, I would be most pleased to answer them. In the interest of time, however, I could make myself available in the coffee shop at the table nearest the lounge, and I would be pleased to answer questions there.

Testifying before Congressional Committees

THE NEXT TIME YOU GET A QUESTION
ON OUR SPENDING , DON'T START
OFF BY SAYING "WOULD YOU BELIEVE..."

ince change is dangerous and progress is the nation's biggest mistake, dedicated bureaucrats in Washington and throughout America should continue the long fight to preserve the values that are the heart of the creative *status quo*. Serving as the bulwark against the encroachments of change, bureaucrats have successfully used the principles of dynamic inaction, and programs of decision postponement, as weapons within the interfacing elements of the executive branch of government.

There are some men and women in the legislative branch, however, who have insisted that the flow of paper be reduced and that there be more action and less study. They have expressed the belief that governmental red tape is strangling both the government and the private sector. Such people fail to appreciate the esthetics of dynamic inaction, and they fail to understand that paper can be beautiful. Red tape can be the tape that binds the nation together as a stable harmonic unit.

Congressman Jim Wright, chairman of the House Public Works Subcommittee on Investigations and Oversight, presided over extensive hearings investigating the red tape involved in the administration of public-works projects. A long parade of witnesses gave their views on "the problem of red tape." An official of the Federal Highway Administration, for example, testified that the environmental-impact statement that is required before construction can begin on highway projects has added an additional 18 million pages of paper annually to the work load of his agency. The state highway engineer of

Alaska stated that he submitted a stack of papers two inches thick on a project for a road three thousand feet long. An official from another state estimated that 50 percent of the man-hours in his state's water-pollution-control office were devoted to processing paper. Witnesses and members of the committee spoke disparagingly of the great flow of paper in the nation.

Invited by Chairman Wright to testify before the committee, the author expressed shock and amazement at the unwarranted and unprecedented attack against red tape and the harmonized increase in the flow of paper.

"What's wrong with paper? After all, do we count the flakes of snow that give a sense of beauty and serenity to the countryside in winter? Do we count the shovel loads of fertilizer that nurture the flowers that brighten our lives? Paper can be beautiful!" Just as a mud-caked sow may be a thing of beauty to a boar, so also a massive flow of multicopy forms and questionnaires may be a thing of grace and beauty to a practicing bureaucrat.

The chief engineer for Texas stated that his draft of an environmental impact statement had to be submitted to sixty-three agencies for comments. Another series of comments, to be filed by the chief engineer, were then required. This kind of inter-agency orchestration of clearances and comments is one of the finest art forms in Washington today. Professional bureaucrats, however, have had to wage a protective battle against reformers who would deny them the freedom of bureaucratic expression. To deny a bureaucrat an opportunity to rhythmically finger tap his way through the mumblistic comments would be to deny him the freedom to be creatively nonresponsive. To eliminate some of the agencies from the commentary orbit would be to remove basic instruments from a great symphony of adjustive concensus.

Senator Thomas McIntyre, chairman of the Senate Subcommittee on Government Regulations, has relentlessly attacked the artistic flow of paper that has been directed to the small entrepreneurs of the country. Investigation by the subcommittee revealed that U.S. businessmen spend $18 billion a year in time and accountants' fees to fill out government forms and return them to agencies of Federal, state, and local government. Another $18 billion is expended each year to print, process, study, and store the 4.5 million cubic feet of paper.

The efforts of Senator McIntyre to "reduce paper work and cut red tape" constitutes yet another effort to assist citizens in their dealings with the government. If this trend continues, the esthetics of red tape may become lost to future generations of probus.

Dedicated probus should stand ready to defend the esthetics of red tape and dynamic inaction in all places and at all times. As an illustration of defensive testimony, a portion of the transcript of hearings on red tape, conducted by the Subcommittee on Investigations and Oversight, House of Representatives, is included for bureaucratic pondering.

The testimony reflects strict adherence to the Boren Guidelines for Bureaucrats: When in charge, ponder. When in trouble, delegate. When in doubt, mumble.

    The author used a three-dimensional organization chart to explain to a congressional committee the need for a cabinet-level department to orchestrate carbon copies of all governmental letters, memoranda, and draft proposals.

N.E.W.S. Photo-News

RED TAPE—INQUIRING INTO DELAYS AND EXCESSIVE PAPERWORK IN ADMINISTRATION OF PUBLIC WORKS PROGRAMS

(92–15)

HEARINGS

BEFORE THE

SUBCOMMITTEE ON
NVESTIGATIONS AND OVERSIGHT

OF THE

,OMMITTEE ON PUBLIC WORKS
HOUSE OF REPRESENTATIVES

NINETY-SECOND CONGRESS

FIRST SESSION

JUNE 15, 16, 17, 22, 23, 24, 1971

RED TAPE—INQUIRING INTO DELAYS AND EXCESSIVE PAPERWORK IN ADMINISTRATION OF PUBLIC WORKS PROGRAMS

TUESDAY, JUNE 22, 1971

House of Representatives,
Subcommittee on Investigations and Oversight
of the Committee on Public Works,
Washington, D.C.

The subcommittee met at 10:06 a.m., pursuant to recess, in room 2253, Rayburn House Office Building, Hon. James C. Wright (chairman of the subcommittee) presiding.

Mr. Wright. The subcommittee will be in order. Today we begin a second week of public hearings on the subject of growing red tape, unnecessary paperwork and costly delays in the Government's Public Works programs. Last week we heard professional testimony to the effect that proliferating guidelines and the ever lengthening review process have added about 4½ years to the timelag before an average stretch of highway can be built and an estimate that this growing delay factor may have added as much as $12 billion to the cost of completing the Federal-aid Highway System. The committee was told that some highway projects must be reviewed and commented upon by as many as 62 different agencies of government, and that one relatively new requirement will add approximately 18 million pages of paperwork annually to the existing load.

We have heard testimony that a typical Corps of Engineers project now consumes approximately 17 years from its congressional inception until the first spadeful of dirt can be turned and the project actually begun.

We were advised that the paperwork necessary to gain approval for a local water pollution abatement effort has tripled in the last 6 years, and that States are having to divert the efforts of professional employees from the vital work of training sewage plant operators and inspecting streams for water quality in order that the time and talents of these people may be consumed in filling out required forms and writing reports.

The committee heard some positive testimony from agencies as to plans for shortening the existing review processes, moving the decisionmaking function closer to the States and the communities affected, but we also have learned that there is a growing tendency among various Federal agencies to set themselves up as rivals and adversaries to one another, and thus to thwart, frustrate, and delay one another's programs.

The committee is in possession of additional material submitted in response to our request for the record by Mr. J. C. Dingwall, State highway engineer for the State of Texas, and without objection, this material as requested by the committee, together with an article in the Houston Post relating to Mr. Dingwall's experience, will be inserted in the record at the point of Mr. Dingwall's testimony.*

Mr. WRIGHT. Our first witness today is Dr. James H. Boren. Doctor Boren is formerly associated with the AID program of the Government, and now is president of the National Association of Professional Bureaucrats.

Doctor Boren, as a formality, and it seems somewhat unnecessary at times, witnesses giving testimony to the subcommittee must be sworn. Therefore, do you solemnly swear that the testimony you will give before this subcommittee will be the truth, the whole truth, and nothing but the truth, so help you God?

Dr. BOREN. Well, more or less. All things are quite relative, you know, and to reduce so complex a matter to a simple categorical response of "yes" or "no" would seem under the circumstances to be thoroughly unprofessional. I would like to ponder your question, Mr. Chairman. It will be recalled that, from early times, those with responsibility for governmental affairs have been wary of the oversimplifications contained in such a question, as witness for example the response of the Roman procurator, Pontius Pilate, who when confronted by a similar question responded with the well-reasoned reply: "What is truth?" If you will permit me to make one point perfectly clear, however, I should like to say that, within the context in which we normally define the relative abstraction of truth, it is expected that the underlying thrust of my testimony will serve the long-range ends foreseen by your question. In the interest of time, since my comment has been so brief, I should like permission to submit for the record a more complete statement on that subject. And I would like to ponder the oath for a while.

Mr. WRIGHT. I have not the faintest idea what the gentleman just said. I think we may defer the question of administering the oath for the time being, and you may proceed in such manner as you desire, Dr. Boren.

STATEMENT OF DR. JAMES H. BOREN, PRESIDENT, NATIONAL ASSOCIATION OF PROFESSIONAL BUREAUCRATS, ACCOMPANIED BY ED EDSTROM, NATAPROBU, CHIEF OF PROTOCOL

Dr. BOREN. Thank you, Mr. Chairman. Mr. Chairman and members of the committee, it is indeed a pleasure to appear before this committee in my capacity as the president and chairman of the Board of the National Association of Professional Bureaucrats.

I am accompanied today by Mr. Ed Edstrom, who serves as the Chief of Protocol of the organization. He brings a wealth of experience to his position with NATAPROBU, which is the acronym for the National Associaton. He is a former president of the National Press Club, and has held key positions in the Justice Department and in the Office of the Chief of Protocol of the U.S. Department of State. He also was

---

*The information referred to appears at page 135.

once associated with a private voluntary organization that has recently gained a hemispheric reputation for its artistry in policy thwartation and implementation postponement.

Mr. WRIGHT. Did you say policy thwartation?

Dr. BOREN. Yes. This is the orbital manner, Mr. Chairman, in which the policy statements laid down by the directive board may be appropriately put into the processes within the vertical system before it is implemented.

I come to these hearings, Mr. Chairman and members of the committee, neither as an adversary to the fine work of this committee nor to the distinguished men who have given previous testimony. I do come to these hearings, however, with heaviness of heart, because I have noted the sustained manner in which the committee has insisted on trying to reduce what it refers to as "redtape" and to eliminate the lengthy delays involved in building highways, dams, and other public works projects.

The committee's insistence on action may cause it to ignore the aesthetics of inaction. It is in this spirit that I welcome the opportunity to discuss the artistic utilization of adjustive procedures and orbital referrals in administrative programing. But first, I think we must look at the question in proper perspective.

Number, quality, and time-related orbital referrals are basic keys to the postponement of decision interfacing, and I believe that this is reflected in the pattern of testimony already presented to this committee. As the president of the National Association of Professional Bureaucrats, I wish to comment on these three postponement keys.

Federal Highway Administrator F. C. Turner, for example, testified that the environmental impact statements required by the National Environmental Policy Act will add approximately 18 million pages of paperwork annually to the burden of his department. But is this so bad? Do we count the flakes of snow that give beauty and a sense of serenity to the countryside in winter? Do we count the drops of rain and shovel-loads of fertilizer that nurture the flowers that brighten our lives and the crops that provide us with food? To move into the numbers game is to establish an impersonal body count in a needless war against bureaucracy.

Mr. WRIGHT. You take the position that paperwork can be beautiful?

Dr. BOREN. Absolutely. I would like to explore that more in depth as we are here in the orbital pattern of the projections today. Instead, Mr. Chairman and members of the committee, I suggest that appropriate consideration be given to the quality of bureaucratic life * * * and that more paper, not less, may be desired. To deny a dedicated fingertapper an adequate supply of paper on which to record the results of his prodigious pondering is to deny him the tools of creative nonresponsiveness. To limit the number of pages on which he is to write is to limit the potential beauty of a sunset. Paper to the professional bureaucrat is as canvas to the artist.

The stress given to the number of pages of paper that flows through the communicative veins of governmental institutions tends to cause the observer to ignore the artistry that can be articulated on a single sheet of paper.

For example, one of the exhibits of this committee—first chart to the left—was a suggested format for the environmental impact statement. The recommended one-page form developed by the Department of the Interior contains 8,800 squares, with each square to be analyzed for appropriateness of reporting. In each instance in which an action crosses with an effect upon the environment, the square is to be divided by a diagonal line to permit the entry of not one but two numbers in each square. An evaluation number (from 1 to 10) indicating the size of the impact is to be entered above the diagonal line, and the evaluation number for the importance of the impact is to be entered below the line. The potential of 17,600 entries on a single page is sufficient to inspire the professional bureaucrat to the level of orbital ecstasy.

Thus, Mr. Chairman, quality of artistry can be found in single pages. But all artists must have freedom to choose their own art form * * * some require massive canvases or reams of paper to express their message in great broad strokes while some artists deal in miniatures and one-page memoranda that embody great detail and beautiful subliminal images.

In considering the factor of timelag, it should be noted that the time between initiation of project proposals and the beginning of project construction is a variable factor from State to State, agency to agency, and project to project. California reported to this committee that the timelag in beginning highway construction has increased from 3 to 6 years in 1961 to 6 to 13 years in 1971.

That is doubling, doubling the timelag in a 10-year period, and it is in keeping with our principles of appropriate pondering. As a matter of fact, to depart from the public works field, Mr. Chairman, I would like to say that we have in NATAPROBU appointed a special committee to look into the possibility of doubling the human gestation period as a contribution to the studies being made on the population problem. If we can move man from a 9-month to an 18-month pregnancy period, we can have a tremendous impact and thereby improve the input-output ratio as they relate to the development problems.

Mr. Dingwall of the Texas State Highway Department testified that the time lag to the point of beginning construction has increased from 44 months in 1961 to 77 months in 1971. After 6 years and 5 months to get to the point of construction, according to his testimony, the highway can be built in 2 years.

I submit that $6\frac{1}{2}$ years or even 13 years is not long to study a project * * * to appropriately scrutinize, analyze, survey, examine, review, contemplate, and ponder. Perhaps with longer study, the problems might disappear; the towns to be served by the proposed highway might die away.

Timelag, carefully orchestrated, may be an important tool in assuring full maturation of projects and often may serve as the powerful but invisible force that substantially provides the apathetic thrust which is essential for maximizing the opportunities for professional ponderers to contemplate the flexible verities that tend to impinge upon the parametrical elements influencing the procedural aspects of decision options.

Creative timelag as applied to the Nation's watershed program illustrates another channel for problem solving by extended processing.

The Deputy Administrator for Watersheds, U.S. Department of Agriculture, testified that the average time required to process the planning and review phase of watershed projects doubled between 1968 and 1970. Doubling in that short a span is even better than what we have experienced with the highways.

In terms of years, the average time between receipt of an application to project completion is now slightly more than 15 years. Here again, longer study and processing may have resolved the problem, because with more time, the remaining land may have washed away.

While the Deputy Administrator indicated his continuing efforts were aimed at reducing the timelag, it is my hope that he may yet see the light and recognize the beauty that reposes in programed delays.

The development of orbital referrals has contributed to the public works field by moving proposals with care through the circular channels of interagency clearances. In the instance of South Lake, Tex., for example, the community leaders were masterfully, I think, spun from Farmers Home Administration to the Department of Housing and Urban Development in its efforts to obtain assistance in a water supply project. This is a case well-known to the distinguished chairman of this subcommittee, Congressman Jim Wright, because he waged a hard fight to stop the spinning and bring one agency to the point of action.

Of course, I am not quite in accord with that. By being judged too large a community for the FHA program and too small a community of the water supply program of HUD, the orbital referral system has operated in the case of original jurisdiction and has been both the practical and esthetic instrument to avoid hasty action. With more time and more study, the problem may resolve itself. The dynamic inaction of the interagency orbital referrals may bring the community to the point of being an overpopulated oasis with an ultimate glory of collapse.

Mr. WRIGHT. Like Rome?

Dr. BOREN. It is a matter of function of time as related to the orbital referral activities that fall within the projected systems on the (mumble. . . . . .).

Mr. WRIGHT. I hope it does not take South Lake as long to get that water supply system as it took Rome to come to its collapse.

Dr. BOREN. You raise a very interesting point, and I would like perhaps to appoint a special committee to look into that.

[Laughter.]

Dr. BOREN. Thus, Mr. Chairman and members of the committee; the factors of number, quality, time, and orbital referrals constitute an ineffable matrix which is in harmony with the principles of the National Association of Professional Bureaucrats. For NATAPROBU seeks to optimize the creative status quo through applying the principles of dynamic inactivism.

Mr. WRIGHT. Dynamic inactivism?

Dr. BOREN. This is the purpose of our organization. By steadfastly adhering to these principles and by fostering the utilization of constructive decision avoidance, we can reduce the rate of program and policy implementation and thus prevent mistakes from being made.

Finally, I do have a specific recommendation to make. I would, if I may, for the record, present a little information on the history of NATAPROBU, and also a copy of the Bureacrat's Soliloquy*, which might serve as an inspiration for those who are concerned with the orbital pattern.

Mr. WRIGHT. Without objection, the material which the gentleman refers to will be inserted in the record.

(The information referred to follows:)

THE HISTORY OF NATAPROBU

The date, April 1, 1968. The occasion, a meeting in the State Department Building in Washington, D.C.,—and the revelation to James H. Boren of the exciting drama to be found in applied dynamic inactivism.

During the first three hours of that historic meeting, Boren was not only bored but also puzzled. He could not understand why the other participants in the meeting seemed so interested in the long, dull, drawn-out proceedings.

"True," Boren reported, "their faces wore the frozen countenance of the professional bureaucrat, but their eyes were sparkling. They were joyously devitalizing ideas with deft thrusts of yes-buttisms and forthright twiddlisms."

"Then came the Gestalt—the aha phenomenon of perception."

"I had viewed the scene as being similar to a boxer punching a bag of mush," Boren said. "It can change its form in response to the boxer's blows, but after the boxer is gone, the bag of mush returns to its old and comfortable shape."

Boren then realized that there can be beauty in a bag of mush and excitement in applying the principles of dynamic inactivism. It was as a missionary seeking to share a new-found revelation that Boren, on May 2, 1968, founded the National Association of Professional Bureaucrats, affectionately known to its members as NATAPROBU.

At the press conference in the National Press Building on May 2, 1968, President Boren announced plans for a NATAPROBU youth program. The Future Bureaucrats of America, and he appointed two committees to develop a course of study for a membership seminar on "Finger-tapping for Promotion and Pleasure." The Bureaucrats Ball of 1967 was held on June 28, 1968, the date on which Standard Form 57 was scheduled for retirement by the U.S. Civil Service Commission. NATAPROBU is continuing its campaign for the return of grand old Standard Form 57 to its place among the great working papers of governmental bureaucracy.

Dr. BOREN. I recommend that a new cabinet level department be created for the purpose of orchestrating the procedural clearances and substantive reviews of all departments and independent agencies of the U.S. Government. The Department of Adjustive Procedures and Orchestrated Clearances (DAPOC) would function through a number of offices and bureaus, but it would also have available as professional resources a number of outstanding men and women who would serve on advisory boards, blue ribbon commissions, and special task forces. Among the bureaus and offices within the new department would be: (1) the Office of Orderly Over-Runs, Permeations, and Statistics (OOOPS); (2) Governmental Linguistic Obtusity Bureau (GLOB);—incidentally, Mr. Chairman, I recall one distinguished gentleman in a department dealing with international development affairs. He was a master of linguistic obtusity. He was able to be extremely creative in the way he could say no. As a matter of fact, day after day and time after time and month after month he was able to say "no" with mere grunts, and I think I may approach him to assist in developing this into a more orbital stage.

---

*The Soliloquy appears at page 365.

Three, Office of Procedural Abstraction Programs (OPAP); (4) Computerized Lethargic Output Division (CLOD); and (5) Management Unit for Maximized Budgetary and Legal Evaluations (MUMBLE).

Of course, these are only a few of the vital offices that need to be established in order to efficiently handle the carbon copies of all correspondence dispatched or received by any Government employee in any governmental office whether in Washington or "in the field."

In order to meet the flexible needs of the new Department of Adjustive Procedures and Orchestrated Clearances, I have developed, Mr. Chairman, with your permission, a three-dimensional organizational chart which shows the manner this can be projected for consideration (indicating).

You will notice this does have great flexibility, because this was designed appropriately. With this flexibility the organization will be able to respond to the issues that may develop within the day. We may also be able to respond in an articulate manner to the processes that are brought (mumble * * *) and we can do this with clarity.

Mr. WRIGHT. You made that point perfectly clear.

Dr. BOREN. You will notice the Secretary is located here in our organizational chart. In many typical charts you will notice that the advisors, the special advisors, are in blocks off to the side. It was our feeling that that was not a functional type of chart, because it did not really show what takes place. Therefore, we have developed our chart so that you do have the orbital screening. These are the special assistants and key advisors who protect the Secretary from the troublesome and unsettling innovative ideas that occasionally may come from a newcomer that comes to the department. So, we do have him appropriately screened.

This [indicating] represents the Office of Public Affairs and Congressional Relations, and you will see that they are normally and positionally in tune. They can translate this appropriately to the key officials within the department. So this represents our basic organizational chart. This of course is the Security Office.

The Security Office is rather flexible also, but you will notice that our structure is such so that in times of great stress, Mr. Chairman, we can move it so that the security man is out front to give the appropriate protection to the organization. We think that this has some special merits for consideration.

Mr. WRIGHT. What is that drooping looking one over in the back?

Dr. BOREN. This is the working employee.

[Laughter.]

Dr. BOREN. This is the deputy coordinator, and here is the coordinator, who coordinates his work.

Mr. WRIGHT. Are you sure you need a working employee?

Dr. BOREN. Mr. Chairman, we try to be democratic. If I may comment, we do have built into this, and we think this is forward looking, which is a great step for us, we have built into this, flexibility for contraction in times of great stress, when there may be some problems, budgetary problems with funding. We can pull certain offices out of existence, and we have given some great thought and consideration to the way and the priorities in which this would be done.

Of course, you would never take away the front office. This is the really important part, because that is the thinking part. One of the last ones we would recommend going would be the one who is carrying the day-to-day burden of the details with which the Secretary and the senior officials should not be concerned. This presents our pattern and our suggestion for the new Department of DAPOC, and I hope, Mr. Chairman, that you may find it possible to support this effort and give us some assistance as we begin now to do our missionary work. We are now going across the land to carry the message of articulate fingertapping and dynamic inactivism to the grassroots of America so they too can become involved in what we consider to be a very relative move.

In summary, I might say that our organization would like to urge the committee to consider that there can be beauty in creative delay, poetry in position postponement, and inspiration in paper artistry. We would say let not insistence on action bring about the destruction of the esthetics of inaction.

I would be very glad to answer any questions.

Mr. WRIGHT. Are there any questions on my right?

Mr. KLUCZYNSKI. Mr. Chairman.

Mr. WRIGHT. Mr. Kluczynski.

Mr. KLUCZYNSKI. I am very much impressed with the statement. I think it is one of the finest I ever heard. I do not know what he is talking about. [Laughter.]

Mr. KLUCZYNSKI. This gadget, was that made by Rube Goldberg?

Dr. BOREN. Actually this was developed by our coordination committee in our shops at Harpers Ferry. We have an office at Harpers Ferry, which is our Office of Committee Orchestration.

Mr. KLUCZYNSKI. Mr. Chairman, way, way back, I was a very good friend of Bob Hope's, when he was in Chicago as a ham actor, and he turned out to be what I thought was one of the greatest actors.

In listening to your testimony this morning, he would not hold a candle to you. Of course, I do not understand this. I have been 41 years in the legislature and business, and I have never heard anything like this in all my life. I was just wondering if you believed what you were saying.

Dr. BOREN. That matter of belief is somewhat like the oath, Congressman. It is a relative thing. The prospects of giving a simple yes or no answer on matters of belief or conviction, but I would like to study that question, and maybe supply an answer for the record, if I may. [Laughter.]

Mr. KLUCZYNSKI. Mr. Chairman, he does not even smile. He is so sincere. [Laughter.]

It is too bad Bella Abzug was not here when you started this thing. It was one of the finest statements. I wish you would look at the gadget over there where the poor working man is way down in left field with the catcher's mitt.

Mr. Chairman, I have no questions. Coming from the stockyards of Chicago, I would not know what he was talking about. It has been a pleasure for me to listen to it.

Mr. ZION. Mr. Chairman.

Mr. WRIGHT. Mr. Zion.

Mr. ZION. Dr. Boren, I have been thoroughly impressed with the orbital transition concept in the testimony, and by the entire synchronized logistical programing process. I think the subcommittee is indebted to you especially for underscoring the integrated management contingencies of this optical management mobility that we are reviewing. [Laughter.]

Mr. ZION. I can only remember one other time that I have been so deeply and completely impressed by a statement. This was a long time ago in China, prior to the time the Communists took over. I was doing some research work. You know in China the eldest, most venerable member of the family is the seat of all wisdom, and one of the oldest and one of the wisest and venerable of all Chinese leaders one time was holding forth at an annual meeting when he tried to give the wisdm of the ages to his progeny, and I remember so well, you reminded me of him.

He sat there in his wisdom countenanced and stringly-beard, and he looked out over the assembly. He said at that time (sentence narrated in Chinese)—I do not understand Chinese. So I never knew what he meant, but I am sure it was about as wise as what we heard today.

Dr. BOREN. I am sure he was very sincere. May I ask a question of the Congressman? Would you consider accepting an advisory position on artistic mumbling?

Mr. ZION. I have been doing this for years.

Dr. BOREN. Following the testimony of the Congressman, I would like to present to you and to the other gentlemen of the committee one of our bureaucrat's executive pencils, which you will notice has an eraser on both ends, and does carry our slogan, "When in doubt, mumble."

We have three basic guidelines in the National Association of Professional Bureaucrats. The first one is "When in charge, ponder." You really do not need to do anything but ponder carefully. The second is, "When in trouble, delegate." The third one is, "When in doubt, mumble."

. . . .

Mr. WRIGHT. Dr. Boren, thank you very much. I wonder if now at this point you would be sworn retroactively at the point at which you began speaking seriously? Do you solemnly swear that the last part of the testimony you have given has been the truth, the whole truth, and nothing but the truth, so help you God?

Dr. BOREN. Yes.

LAPSE OF TIME

APPLICATION RECEIVED TO PLANNING AUTHORIZATION

PL 566 WATERSHED PROTECTION PROGRAM

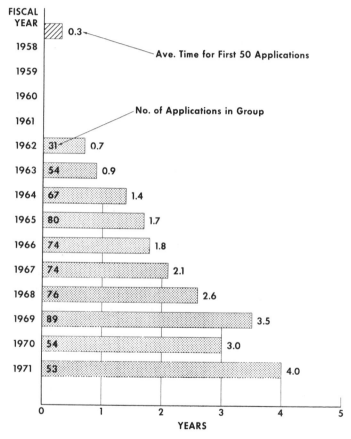

As of July 1, 1970, 2,885 applications had been submitted to the Washington office for Federal assistance in watershed planning. Applications for assistance under the Act may be submitted by any qualified local organization. Applications must be approved by the State approving agency.

The chart shows a sustained rate of submission of applications for assistance during thirteen years but a decrease in rate during 1968, 1969, and 1970.

During the past Fiscal year 50 applications were authorized for work plan development. This brought the total watersheds authorized for planning assistance to 1,561. Planning has been suspended or terminated in a total of 192 watersheds. These suspensions or terminations were at the request of the local organizations or with their concurrence.

LAPSE OF TIME

OPERATIONS APPROVAL TO PROJECT COMPLETION

FISCAL YEAR **PL 566 WATERSHED PROTECTION PROGRAM**

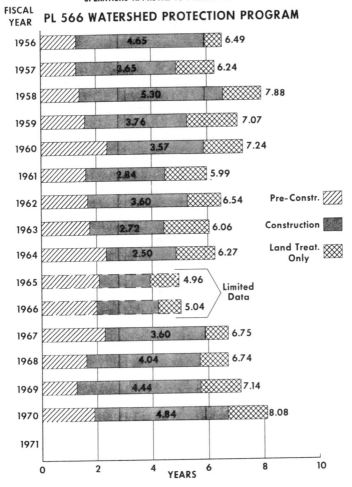

This chart shows the progress in Public Law 566 installations. On July 1, 1970, 1,001 projects had been approved for the installation of planned measures. The work in progress in the projects includes surveys, investigations, preparation of detailed designs, specifications and engineering cost estimates for construction of structural work. It also includes technical assistance for applying land treatment for watershed protection.

The project construction stage begins with the execution of the first project agreement or Federal contract for construction of structural works of improvement, which obligates the government to furnish its share of the construction costs. By July 1, 1970 initial project agreements between the local sponsoring organizations and the Soil Conservation Service had been executed on 724 of these projects. Construction was underway on 433 projects and had been completed on 291.

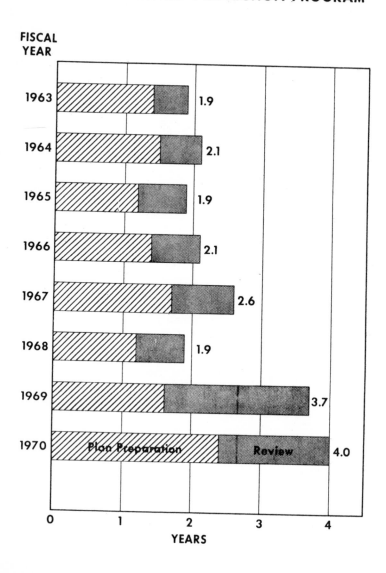

LAPSE OF TIME
PLANNING AUTHORIZED TO OPERATIONS APPROVAL
PL 566 WATERSHED PROTECTION PROGRAM

2
Academic
and Corporate
Thrumming

The Dangers of Communication

chapman

round the bridge tables of America, the bargaining tables of management and labor, and the conference tables of negotiating diplomats, attention is focused today on the *need to communicate*. The fact that there may not be anything of significance to communicate is, of course, irrelevant to the need and the form of communication.

A senior official of the Federal Government opened an address to a group of civil-service employees with the statement: "We must bring people together, and this we can do by communicating." A political candidate once spoke of the need to bring people together, and togetherness has been a theme on college campuses throughout the nation.

Probus should never oppose bringing people together, because that is the first step in organizing a committee or establishing a study group. The danger flag to the bureaucrat is not in togetherness or the form of communication but in the degree to which substance may be involved in the formal or informal discussion agenda after people have been brought together. To introduce substance to communication is to invite differing views and disharmony to the bureaucratic scene.

Many of the problems of the world today can be traced to the fact that there is too much communication, not too little.

COMMUNICATIVE EXCESSES

Because wives have communicated with wives, neighborhoods have been disrupted. When the morning coffee session in a neighborhood results in a wife learning that her husband was seen slipping out of a topless restaurant or being given a speeding ticket, the tranquil seas of matrimony may be disturbed. When conversation at a morning bridge party turns to the sighting of a neighbor's car at a suburban motel, explosive charges may be triggered. What constructive purpose, one might ask, can be served when wives indiscriminately discuss husbandly inclinations toward topless restaurants, exotic massage parlors, and nonchurch bingo parties?

Neighborhoods characterized by ease of communication are neighborhoods that are flirting with disaster. Neighborhoods that have freedom of movement but absence of communication, on the other hand, are neighborhoods that are likely to remain peaceful and contribute to the image of a moral America.

Because secretaries have communicated intimately with their bosses, families have been torn apart. Many secretaries are artists in communication, and they may express their artistry in terms of low-cut blouses, flattering skirts, and bra-less profiles. A pendulous walk may be accompanied by flashing smiles and friendly side glances. Advanced stages of secretarial communication may involve night work sessions on annual reports or secretarial assistance on out-of-town conventions and sales meetings. Optimized communication and warm understanding ultimately may result in modification of familial organization charts. Limited communication between secretary and boss, however, may preserve the *status quo* in both home and office. The development of the women's liberation movement will have little effect on the nature of the secretary-to-boss communication dangers. Though the female secretary-to-male-boss may give way to male secretary-to-female-boss in terms of sexist identity, the basic nature of the communication danger will tend to remain constant.

When soldiers have easily communicated with members of Congress, investigations have been launched and appropriations have been reduced. The sanctity of the chain of command has been subjected to ignoble neglect by enlisted men and many junior officers in the modern army. The disregard for established report procedures in the military complex has resulted in a great flow of information from the soldiers on the fields of combat. The information may not be in full harmony with the information handouts from the dedicated information officers at headquarters. Such increased communication has resulted in charges of atrocities and a series of courts-martial. Public reaction and congressional indignation have been disconcerting by-products of direct communication.

The greatest threat to the milicrats,[1] therefore, has not been on the fields of battle but in the halls of Congress. Congressional committees have increasingly demanded to know more about military programs and military expenditures. In some instances, the Congress has even made moves to reduce the level of funds appropriated for military-assistance programs and international war games.

Greater adherence to established channels and procedures can control the communication pattern of soldiers and prevent embarrassment to the military leadership of the nation. Potential embarrassment can be equated with threat to the national security.

Political leaders who have communicated honestly with their constituents have run the risk of defeat at the polls. Holders of public office often try to explain complicated issues to their constituents in logical terms that are honest but involved. Their reward may well be defeat.

Political bureaucrats should never seek to inform or educate their constituency, and the use of logic is dangerous. The professional political bureaucrat (polibu) should communicate in carefully developed terms that are consistent with emotional intertwining.[2] Polibus who have been successful in the political arena are those who have communicated their name without communicating substantive views on issues. Those who have made the mistake of communicating honestly without balancing the communication with high emotivity and flamboyant timing will ultimately depart the center of the arena.

The Nixon announcement of Dr. Kissinger's work as an international advance man was an effective emotive device, because it involved the artistry of executive stealth. It was political application of the P.T. Barnum principle that people like to be fooled. The Nixon announcements on wage- and price-control decisions are another illustration of shellistic communications.[3] Emotivity and timing! The Nixon war-withdrawal program gives strong hints that the real Nixon plan for Laos is the methadone treatment for an adjustive withdrawal from Vietnam.

[1]The term "milicrat" was first used by John Cramer of *The Washington Daily News* to describe the professional bureaucrats of the military complex.

[2]Professional political bureaucrats, polibus, differ from other probus essentially in the fact their rating on performance is done by *people* on Election Day. The polibus (pronounced *polybooze*), therefore, have a unique set of clearing procedures and a different focus on communication.

[3]Shellistic communication is characterized by skillful obfuscation of: (1) policy elements, and (2) policy authorship. The term is derived from a game played by the traveling artisans of American road shows.

Excessive communication between office holder and voter may result in political defeat.

When corporate officers have communicated details of development plans and merger possibilities to the company's officers, unsettling questions may lead to a change in corporate management. Full disclosure of management plans and problems is often proposed by beginning corporate bureaucrats in the belief that stockholders should have some influence on the decisions of the company. Experienced corporate bureaucrats, however, know that full communication between management and stockholders can result only in problems.

Citizens who insist on communicating new ideas to the heads of governmental agencies are the greatest disturbing factor with which governmental bureaucrats must deal. Bureaucratic tranquillity is disturbed even more when the citizens channel their ideas for innovative programs or procedures through their representatives in the Congress. But, since the citizens who insist on communicating with the governmental agencies normally deal with matters or experiences relating to their business or profession, they may unknowingly reveal information that may lead to negative governmental action.

Consider, for example, the experience of an inventor who devoted time, effort, and money in trying to develop a new type of rotor for a helicopter. Ultimately communicating with the Federal Aviation Administration through a front-page newspaper photograph and story, he found that his six-inch tethered flight brought him not glory but anguish in the form of charges that could have netted him a two-thousand-dollar fine. He failed to have prior authorization to penetrate the earth's air space by six inches. The fact that his craft was tethered and not in free flight removed the matter from FAA jurisdiction. The inventor's efforts to communicate with FAA officials had been to little avail until the newspaper established the contact. Thus, when communication *was* established, problems developed.

Consider the case of the milk routeman who shared with his company the methods he used to increase the number of customers on his route, and was rewarded with his route being halved. Or, think of a man who developed a local mail-delivery system more efficient and less costly than the official postal service. Excessive communication about his system and his utilization of private stamps resulted in governmental action that altered his business.

When a Pentagon man communicated honestly with a committee of the Congress about the cost factors of a military project, he was fired.

Professional bureaucrats, therefore, should be ever alert to the dangers of *substantive* communication. They should develop skills that will help them change emphasis on substance into emphasis on form. For example, when a citizen group meets to initiate policy reform, the probu should divert the discussion from policy issues to involved discussion of organizational by-laws. If he is able to drag the discussion into several hours, the substantive issues either will never be raised or they will be raised after the reformers are no longer alert. In emergencies, or when surprise issues are raised, the probu should insist on putting the problem in its proper perspective. Such a move provides the mechanism for diluting attention that may be directed to the heart of the issue and perhaps trigger mechanisms for form-oriented debate.

Assume, for example, that an attempt is being made to abolish the bureau in the Pentagon that is in charge of the inventory and polishing of musket flints. The probu should immediately move to put the issue into its proper perspective. The history of the *bureau* can be traced to the period of the revolutionary war and the importance of army tradition can be woven into a long and majestic tapestry of fringeful communication.[4] By tracing the long history of musketry and flints, opportunities may develop to move the discussion into other related fields. Such a wide-ranging discussion will permit perspective to replace substance in the agenda and thus help postpone the development of specific recommendations until future meetings.

PEOPLE CAN KNOW TOO MUCH

When citizens know what a government agency is doing or about to do, problems can result. An expressway to be built through a park, rezoning to permit construction of high-rise apartments adjacent to historical landmarks, or plans to permit massive timber cutting in national forests are but illustrative of the type of public business that should be shielded from the public if bureaucracy and fiscal harmony are to prevail.

When people know too much about their public business, they may want to get involved. They may want to express disruptive opinions and may try to impose themselves upon the delicately balanced internal workings of a bureau or office. They may wish to

[4]Creekmore Fath of Austin, Texas, has made a long and interesting study of Twain's flint-picking approach to the four-year cycle of Federal employment.

express opinions on war and other matters best left in the hands of the White House bureaucrats who are expert in the field. Citizens may learn enough about the problems of pollution that they may wish to stir Congress to take stronger action in the form of effective pollution laws. At times, they may even want to preserve seashores and public lands for public use.

One of the greatest problems with which bureaucrats are confronted is the myth that people have a right to know something about their own public business. An even greater set of problems evolves from the occasional insistence that people should actually have a voice in the governmental decisions affecting them. Such thinking tends to subvert impressionable beginning bureaucrats and undermine the security of governmental bureaucracy itself.

It is imperative, therefore, that the amount and substance of information made available to the public be carefully screened. Despite the best efforts of governmental administrators to control them, most information officers have a news media background and are inclined to give inordinate amounts of substantive information to the public. Bureau chiefs should establish safeguards that will assure that all press releases are scrutinized and sanitized before they are distributed.

No professional bureaucrat should publicly approve censorship, but, of course, no probu should ever make public any information that in some future era could be embarrassing or threaten the national security. Since it is difficult to measure the long-range security effects of general information on programs and recommendations, the probu should classify most of the internal memoranda and documents with which he works. With study and practice, the probu can learn to equate career security with national security. Experienced governmental bureaucrats follow a simple rule on security matters: When in doubt, classify.

Another means of controlling excessive disclosure of substantive information to the public is the previously described use of professional terminology. Governmental bureaucrats and lawyers use a special terminology that blends the best of the procedural with the best of the legal terminology. Particularly useful are references to codes and titles. The Foreign Assistance Act, for example, provides the basis for probus to talk about "Title 9" programs, and the Civil Aeronautics Board mixes references to "single entity" and "pro rata" aspects of "207 provisions" on charter flights.[5] An official

---

[5]Single-entity charter flights are charters in which the cost of air transportation is paid by an organization or a single entity; passengers make no payment for transportation. Pro-rata charters are those in which the members of a group pay for their pro-rata share of the charter flight.

of the Department of Housing and Urban Development has described the references to titles and codes as the "shorthand" of departmental communication.

Academic bureaucrats at one time dialogued on apperceptive mass and curriculum enrichment. Subsequent educational thrust has shifted from workshops on core-curricula features to discussions on grants, foundation proposals, GRE, ACT, and the interfacing of the AFT and the NEA.

TO GET ALONG, GO ALONG

"To get along, go along" remains today the counsel that new members of Congress receive when they arrive on Capitol Hill. The sanctity of tradition and the importance of the unwritten rules of the Hill are quickly learned by freshmen members if they are to properly represent their constituents. Nothing is more sacred in the Congress, however, than the manner in which leadership is developed through the process of seniority. To become a leader on Capitol Hill, a member must adapt to the tested and proven processes. Congressional seniorization, like homogenization, tends to disperse the disruptive elements of virgin material. To get along, go along.

In the student world, it is the homogenized student who will receive the greatest products of the educational system, the products of grades and honors. With the exception of the nonacademic nocturnal studies, grades tend to be the chief aim of the student.

Professors and particularly department heads quickly identify the students in their classes that possess the attributes of harmonized docility that mark the true scholar. Students who disrupt professors' lectures by asking probing questions in search of knowledge are violating the principles of harmonized docility. If students must ask questions, they should ask them in a puzzlistic fashion as the professor and student stroll from the classroom.

A student may properly say to the professor, "I have been unable to understand the importance of three-letter words in Shakespeare's *Hamlet*. Do you believe, Professor, that. . . .?" Questions of belief are safer to ask than questions of fact.[6] If a question of fact *must*

---

[6]Identity questions are helpful to both students and professors. These are questions that a student asks after class, not for the purpose of information but for the purpose of identifying to the professor. This helps the student indicate for grading purposes that he is a serious student, and it helps the professor identify the person who may create an unpleasant scene if a good grade is not given.

be asked, certainly it should be posed in the post-class stroll, because it will enable the professor to: (1) prodigiously ponder the matter and consider the full implications of the question, and (2) look it up.

FAILSAFE TEACHING AND FAILSAFE LEARNING

Communication between students and professors should be carefully orchestrated. Professors primarily should transmit to their students the information that was transmitted to them by their professors. Information that has stood the test of the ages and has moved from professors' notebooks to students' notebooks can be viewed as safe and nondisruptive. The multigeneration transmittal of information from notebook to notebook can be termed "failsafe teaching" and "failsafe learning."

Students should play their assigned role in the educational process and gratefully accept the information that the professor, in his professional wisdom, believes to be good for the student. Students who do not accept their role in the harmonizing homogenization of the learning process will not receive the grades or the honors that reflect academic success to parents and employers.

Professors who violate the principles of failsafe teaching fail to meet their responsibility to serve as an instrument of the *status quo*. This is particularly true in the social sciences, where students may learn more than is good for them to know. Administrators and trustees should serve with responsible professors as the guardians of educational integrity and should protect students and society in general from the unsettling interplay of ideas.

Students who reject the principles of failsafe learning are violating their responsibility to their parents and society when they insist on probing for knowledge. A little learning may be dangerous but more learning may be catastrophic. When students accept harmonizing homogenization, they will find their rewards in better grades, more honors, and institutional and taxpayer acceptability.

When substance is filtered from communication, societal tranquillity will not be endangered. Skillfully blending professional terminology with the security aspects of classification helps the professional bureaucrats meet their high national responsibility.

Regardless of what political philosophers may write in their great works, the professional bureaucrats know that they are collectively the ultimate repository of national values.

Academic
Artisans

hrough the ages, academic bureaucrats (aca-bus, pronounced *acka-booze*) have made major contributions to the world's second-oldest profession. Their mastery of grantsmanship knows no equal, and their skill in semantical projections is matched only by senior practitioners in the Pentagon complex.

For example, a professor, now at a university in the Midwest, wrote a major treatise entitled *Syntax-Semantics Systems as Structure Manipulation Systems: Phrase Structure Grammars and Generalized Finite Automata.* To explain the thrust of his study, the professor wrote, "Given a syntactically ambiguous grammar, it is possible to use semantic information to disambiguate its syntax and construct a similar unambiguous grammar."[1] Probus in the corporate and governmental bureaucracies would do well to study semantical prolusions as a means of developing nonresponsive communications mechanisms.[2]

While practicing probus should give verbal support to all efforts to disambiguate syntax, they should not actually

[1]Buttlemann, H. William, *Syntax-Semantics Systems as Structure Manipulation Systems: Phrase Structure Grammars and Generalized Finite Automata.* A Ph.D. dissertation, the University of North Carolina, 1970.

[2]Neo-Chomskycally speaking, a sentence constructurally multiplistic by virtue of syntactical rules operating without reference to semantical differentiation may be classified by utilizing semantical cues inherent in the linguistic communication situation under consideration. Such semantical cues serve to identify the proper underlying phrase-marker initially obfuscated by the transformational shifting of form-classes in the lineal generation of the undisambiguated phrase-marker.

implement disambiguational programs. To do so would undermine two of the most basic of all bureaucratic art forms, vertical mumbling and semantical qualification.

Academicians also have made notable contributions to the state of the bureaucratic art in procedural as well as semantical endeavors. Student registration procedures at colleges, for example, reflect effective collaboration by faculty and administration officials in introducing students to the sanctity of established channels. Though the system may vary from institution to institution, the students quickly learn that planning and logic are matters for classroom discussion, not a basis for campus operations.

Students must master the forms, decipher the course offerings, and learn the sequence-maze that will enable them to find faculty advisers at a table in the gymnasium or in some departmental office. Patience, hope, and charity are taught the students as they experience special meditation periods while waiting to have their course cards initialed or have their money accepted. Variety is occasionally added when computer cards are used, and special artistry may be introduced when the cards are color coded for the clearances used in previous registration periods but no longer in use. The optimal level of procedural instruction is reached, however, when students learn that class sections that fit their schedule needs are filled, and they must begin the course-card process anew.

Academic bureaucrats must master the internal procedures of the school system or university, and they should also learn the relationship between the internal organization factors and those of the academic constituency. Academic probus must learn that when they teach students they also communicate with parents and the business community. To gain a reputation as a fine teacher, a probu should be more concerned with classroom discipline and meeting administrative report deadlines than with teaching students. A teacher who, in addition to having a quiet classroom, avoids current and local controversies has the mark of the successful academic probu.[3]

GRADES AND STUDENT PERFORMANCE

At the elementary, secondary, and college level, the academic probu must master the art of rating student performance. Grades, however,

[3]Probus in academe can cautiously discuss matters that are controversial if the matters are distant in terms of (1) geography and (2) time.

need not reflect performance and certainly need not reflect learning. Grades or marks are the subjective reflection of an objective tool. Since grades are primarily for parents, the probu can use them as an instrument of classroom control. Threats of downgrading for disciplinary breaches and the use of classroom study periods for memorization of isolated facts can help maintain the quiet classroom that will make the teacher appear competent in the eyes of most administrators.

The more complicated a grading system, the less second-guessing a teacher will have from parents. The Elementary School Progress Report 1-6 that is used by the Fairfax County School System in Virginia, for example, provides for sixty-one reporting items plus space for teacher comments. A first-grade student can be marked for making "commendable progress," "satisfactory progress," or "not making expected progress."

Among the items for grading are "Selects Appropriate Procedures to Formulate, Analyze, and Solve Problems (Stated or Observed) Involving: Whole Numbers and Operations; Introduction to Integers"; or, "Perceives Through Emotional and Intellectual Involvement"; and another, "Gains a Working Knowledge of Major Social Studies Concepts Through Application of the Following Skills: Using Time and Spatial Relationships." With sixty-one items as potential grading elements, the teacher in Fairfax County, Virginia, can fuzzistically project an interface avoidance stance when parents seek an explanation of grades. The technique is particularly helpful when the probu cannot remember the names and faces of students and cannot match students to parents.

Some teachers and principals in Fairfax County, Virginia, and elsewhere in the nation are beginning to insist on directing classroom efforts away from grades and toward student learning. Such trends should be quashed by academic probus at every opportunity, because they will tend to disturb the equilibrium of the academic vessel.

PRESIDENTIAL SEARCH COMMITTEE

Another illustration of academic thrumming is the putteristic pattern that is used for the selection of college presidents.

The presidential-search committee is not only a delightful mechanism for decision postponement but also an effective means of diffusing decision-making responsibility. Typically, the board of trustees of a college appoints a search committee composed of two or three of its own members, faculty representatives, student leaders, and citizens at large. The committee may solicit applications and nominations, but, of course, this is not done until the appropriate committee and subcommittee studies have been made to determine the type of president the search committee thinks the college should have. To assist it in defining the goals and objectives of the search committee's search, some committees hire consultants to tell the committee what the committee wants.

It is quite common for committees to select a consultant whose views are known, and whose views, therefore, may coincide with those of the committee members. The consultant's recommendations tend to give added legitimacy and authority to the committee's decisions. They also may serve as an objective buffer to subsequent criticism.

The use of consultants to tell one what one wishes to hear is a well-known bureaucratic technique that can be termed "echosulting."[4] The process of echosulting is normally that of dittoanalysis. A consultant may become an echosultant through his selection by those knowing his professional work. In such instances, he may unknowingly fill the role of the echosultant. There may be other instances, however, in which a professional echosultant who employs dittoanalysis is selected as a result of cautious and collaborative negotiation. Presidential-search committees tend to prefer echosultants to assist them both in defining their goals and in the final selection of a president.

The files of presidential "candidates" are meticulously screened and prodigiously pondered. Survivors of the paper screening process may or may not be notified of their survival status; losers normally will read about the final selection in the newspapers. Subsequent preliminary interviews conducted by a subcommittee of the search committee may lead to "finalist" interviews with all members of the search committee participating.

When the presidential-search committee makes its recommendations to the board of trustees, the board may finger tap its way through the recommendations, and hire whomever it planned to hire anyway. Nine to eighteen months may pass while the searchers search. There have been recorded instances in which the echosul-

---

[4]Echosulting is used extensively by governmental and corporate bureaucrats. It is particularly useful in gaining support for a weak position.

tant to the search committee was hired. With views and philosophy in tune with those of the committee, the echosultant may also have been the only person known to the committee who could articulately mumble the combined terminology of administrators, professors, students, and fund raisers. Probus in other fields have learned much from the presidential-search techniques of academe.[5]

While the search for a college or university president offers the greatest opportunities of orchestrating bureaucratic programmation, the search for college deans also opens doors for committee operations. The Search Committee for Dean of Faculty of St. Mary's College of Maryland, for example, advertised in the *New York Times* for applicants. The qualifications of the dean for which the search committee was searching were professionally pondered and properly written. The advertisement read:

> The College is committed to a consultative process of decision making in Academic affairs in an attempt to minimize the possibility of conflict inherent in a hierarchical structure and to maximize the opportunity for cooperative participation in constructive decision making. The Faculty has primary leadership in the formulation of all academic policies, which, through systematic procedures of consultation among all interested groups, are ultimately established by the Board of Trustees. The role of Dean of Faculty in this context is not to make final decisions regarding policy determination but rather to strengthen the consultative process by coordinating the activities of Faculty and Administration, facilitating communication, and providing necessary information. The Dean also has full responsibility for the implementation of established policy and administration of Academic affairs including the areas of General Planning, Personnel, Curriculum, Teaching and Learning, and Budget.[6]

Interested applicants were invited to address correspondence to the chairman of the search committee. Corporate and governmental

[5]The presidential-search techniques of academe have so effectively placed the decision-making process in fuzzistic orbit that some of them have been adopted by the White House and the Civil Service Commission. The avoidance mechanisms in the executive talent search are coordinated with the party's national committee, senatorial campaign committee, and congressional campaign committee. State party chairmen and state representatives on the national committee of the party are also part of the nomination-clearance orchestration. This substructural contribution of the academic world to the governmental realm reflects once again that a bureaucrat can no longer be defined merely as an employee of a governmental bureau.

[6]*New York Times,* Sunday, April 2, 1972.

bureaucrats who write job descriptions for responsible administrators should study the descriptive art of academe.

PUBLISH OR PERISH

While the presidential- and dean-of-faculty search committee process reflects adherence to bureaucratic procedures, the functioning of academic councils, faculty committees, interdepartmental committees, student committees, and faculty sponsorship of student activities also reflects steadfast devotion to the sanctity of established channels. Since professors and deans at institutions of higher learning are both products and producers, a major effort is made to assure an orderly continuity of the cycle of student-to-professor status. As a part of this process of training students to become professors, particular attention is given to pedantic research and publishing. The students are required to write papers about matters so narrowly defined that the students will become accustomed to the publishing game of academe.

A dissertation was written at the University of Missouri entitled *The Effect of Expectation-Press Incongruency on Junior College Transfer Student Achievement.* Another, at the University of Pittsburgh, was presented as *A Study of the Differences between the Concept of the Nature of Mathematics Held by Freshmen and That Held by College Faculty.* Also at the University of Pittsburgh was a study with the title, *An Examination of the Diversity of Approaches to Problems by Successful and Non-Successful Problem Solvers Enrolled in a Non-Calculus Introductory College Physics Course.* The University of Florida made its contribution with a dissertation, *An Investigation of Programs of Community Action in Urban Community Colleges as Implementations of the Community Services in Junction of the Community College Philosophy.* Dissertations provide the training by which future professors may retain their positions. Most institutions of higher learning require that their professors write books or write articles for the "learned journals." Failure to "publish" means failure to be promoted up the professorship ladder. Regardless of the professor's ability to teach, the rule is *up* or *out,* and the only way *up* is to publish.

University administrators and promotion committees indicate a high degree of bureaucratic reverence to form and institutional image by their "publish or perish" rule for professors. Scholarly study and scientific research are functions of a university, but promotion committees and administrators are more influenced by a body count of publications than they are with the substantive contributions to the fund of knowledge. Related to the publication rule, of course, are the public-relations and grant attraction factors. An institution with a favorable public image will attract more funds from the public and private sectors than will an institution that places great emphasis on the humdrum quality of superior teaching.

THE LANGUAGE OF ACADEME

Acabus have developed a specialized language that should inspire other bureaucrats to greater effort either in the written or mumblistic projections. While most people tend to think that the purpose of language is to communicate, the academic artisans have developed a set of terms and phrases that enable educators to communicate with educators without communicating with anyone else. This is a great contribution to professional survival, because it avoids disruptive incursions from parents and taxpayers who may want to raise questions about educational programs that impinge upon the children of the nation.

While it is true that other probus have their own language of specialization, none can match the skill of the educators in interlacing word modifiers with marginal thoughts. A layman can unmask the semantical cover of lawyers, and children can master the terminology of the complicated dialoguing of space scientists. But only an educator can understand an educator! And there have been instances in monitored workshops when classroom teachers could not communicate with distinguished university professors.

A great threat to the sanctity of academe has been made in the form of dictionaries and glossaries that can fall into the hands of mere people. While it may be argued that the glossaries have been developed to facilitate communication between educators, the argument is based on the questionable assumption that educators *should* communicate with each other. Certainly, if glossaries are to be developed for professional use, they should be kept out of the hands of parents and taxpayers.

For the parent who wants to know how his or her child is doing in school, the professional terms may be somewhat confusing, but it is the price to pay for citizen noninterference in educational programs. A parent, for example, might read an article referring to the use of magazines in training or learning experiments. The parent might visualize a group of students reading *Playboy* or studying fold-outs of some woman's magazine. "Magazine," to the educator, however, is defined as "a mechanical device that delivers reinforcers to an organism during periods of reinforcement." "Magazine training" is "subjecting the experimental organism to the apparatus that delivers the reinforcer until such time when it approaches the delivery mechanism and takes the reinforcer each time it is operated without a display of disruptive emotional behavior."[7]

Professional terminology cannot only protect the ramparts of academe from unsettling questions from laymen, it *can* protect educators from educators. Imagine also the great excitement in a national conference of teachers when a group of professors on a panel begin to dialogue on manipulanda, across-the-bottom synchronization, interorganismic generality, and extinction ratio. The terms, of course, have no reference to sex, paddling, or Vietnam, but they can screen the real subject of the panel from visiting school-board members or members of the legislature.

As in other fields of bureaucratic endeavor, the acabus can speak in acronyms and professional shorthand. Simple phrases such as "inter-reinforcement time" become ISRT, "conjugate schedule" becomes CONJG (has nothing to do with verbs), and "intra-response time" is translated into IRAT.[8] The areas of academic communication and related teacher behavior remain to be studied with respect to TO (time out) and threshold penumbra.[9]

CONCLUSION

Successful acabus should not waste time, knowledge, and communicative talent by focusing on such student-oriented frills as teaching.

[7]Owen R. White, *A Glossary of Behavioral Terminology* (Champaign, Illinois: Research Press Company, 1971), p. 90.

[8]According to informed sources in Harpers Ferry, West Virginia, a group of graduate students has received a grant from a mattress manufacturer to conduct a study relating to IRAT. IRAT, for intra-response time, is the time that elapses between the commencement of a response and its termination or completion. It is believed that the study of bedwetting patterns of infants may result in a major revolution in the mattress industry. The IRAT of bedwetting, however, will not be directed toward the use of water beds.

[9]TO, for time out, has no reference to sporting events or coffee breaks. TO can be defined as an "operation" or as a "process." As an operation, it deals with removing an organism from a situation where reinforcement or punishment is available, or noticeably withholding or suspending the reinforcement or punishment contingencies for a short period of time.

Their pursuit of scholarly research should not be guided by a search for knowledge but for the possible discovery of uncharted educational terrain that might offer a new opportunity to place a new term or acronym on the map of knowledge. The acabus should "publish"; they should make the speaking circuit of civic clubs, parent-student-teacher associations, and television talk shows. They should plow the foundation and governmental fields in hopes of harvesting a financial crop to support more grant-oriented research and more promotion-oriented publications.

Of such academic quality are sustained The Movement and the brotherhood of bureaucracy.

Corporate Twiddling

SHORT RADIUS
REFERRAL
(TWIDDLISM)

LONG RADIUS.
ORBITAL REFERRAL

hile corporate bureaucrats may have learned much from governmental bureaucrats, there are today many lessons that the corporate practitioners can teach their governmental counterparts. Appropriate channels, status-oriented protocol, orbital referrals, and twiddlisms are among the decision postponement factors utilized by corporate bureaucrats.

A major transportation company reinforces the status position of its executives by its rules on internal memoranda. A memo written, for example, by one executive to an executive who is his senior must address the memo to Mr. Executive from Executive.

If the memo is to a person junior to the writer, the memo is to be addressed to Executive from Mr. Executive. Inappropriate salutation has resulted in an interception and return of the memo by the staff of the communications secretariat. Short-radius referrals of this type can be described as "twiddlisms."

Twiddlisms in series can be as effective as the larger and slower-moving orbital referrals (the long-radius referrals) in the action-avoidance programs.

TWIDDLISTIC OPPORTUNITIES

Twiddlisms in series is an avoidance mechanism that can be used by small or large organizations of all types of bureaucratic institutions. Though the academic and governmental bureaucracies utilize twiddlisms to good effect, the corporate practitioners have the greatest range of twiddlistic opportunities.

A high-school student in the Washington area ordered new musical equipment from a national retail company. Time was important to the student, because he had an opportunity to join a rock group that was to play at high-school and neighborhood parties. The promised four-day delivery date was changed time after time. Twiddlisms in series came into play, and an inspirational postponement design was soon evident.

Two months after the student had placed his order for the equipment, the National Association of Professional Bureaucrats advised the company that it had been nominated for the Order of the Bird. The nomination unfortunately broke the series. The company substituted more expensive equipment and made immediate delivery.

The artistry of twiddlistic series is projected in Organogram Number Three C/Gamma.

INSTRUMENT OF ORBITAL REFERRAL

While the long-radius or orbital referrals have been a major instrument of governmental bureaucracies, the corporate world has made use of the technique as well. The insurance industry, for example, has developed the orbital-referral system to the point that legitimate claims may be in equatorial motion for two or more years before a decision is made. The case of a Virginia man whose car was struck by another car is a typical illustration.[1]

The driver of offending Car B stated that he was forced to plunge into Victim Car A because Car C, a third vehicle, had moved from the curb into his lane. The innocent victim was first assured of immediate payment by the adjuster for Crawford and Company, but later was advised that he would have to await the decision of the insurance industry's Inter-Company Arbitration Committee. The arbitration committee would decide whether the driver of Car B or Car C was responsible for the accident and thus which insurance company would pay for the repair of Victim Car A.

Nine months passed before the arbitration committee made the determination that the driver of Car C was responsible. The driver of Victim Car A then contacted State Farm Mutual Automobile Insurance Company, the company adjudged by the arbitration committee to be responsible for payment of the claim. The claim representa-

---

[1]Crawford and Company; Falls Church, Virginia, Office; Claim Number 8A-363645-8, Crawford file number 66-44222-WO. State Farm Insurance Companies claim number 46-4244-405.

ORGANOGRAM THREE C/GAMMA: DELIVERY POSTPONEMENT FLOW CHART/RETAIL

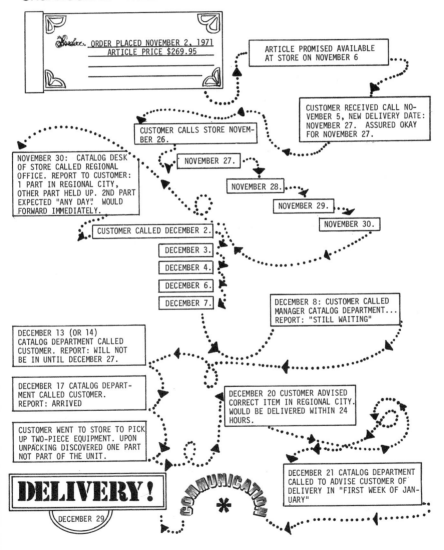

ORDER PLACED NOVEMBER 2, 1971
ARTICLE PRICE $269.95

ARTICLE PROMISED AVAILABLE
AT STORE ON NOVEMBER 6

CUSTOMER RECEIVED CALL NO-
VEMBER 5, NEW DELIVERY DATE:
NOVEMBER 27. ASSURED OKAY
FOR NOVEMBER 27.

CUSTOMER CALLS STORE NOVEM-
BER 26.

NOVEMBER 30: CATALOG DESK
OF STORE CALLED REGIONAL
OFFICE. REPORT TO CUSTOMER:
1 PART IN REGIONAL CITY,
OTHER PART HELD UP. 2ND PART
EXPECTED "ANY DAY". WOULD
FORWARD IMMEDIATELY.

NOVEMBER 27.

NOVEMBER 28.

NOVEMBER 29.

NOVEMBER 30.

CUSTOMER CALLED DECEMBER 2.

DECEMBER 3.

DECEMBER 4.

DECEMBER 6.

DECEMBER 7.

DECEMBER 8: CUSTOMER CALLED
MANAGER CATALOG DEPARTMENT...
REPORT: "STILL WAITING"

DECEMBER 13 (OR 14)
CATALOG DEPARTMENT CALLED
CUSTOMER. REPORT: WILL NOT
BE IN UNTIL DECEMBER 27.

DECEMBER 17 CATALOG DEPART-
MENT CALLED CUSTOMER.
REPORT: ARRIVED

DECEMBER 20 CUSTOMER ADVISED
CORRECT ITEM IN REGIONAL CITY.
WOULD BE DELIVERED WITHIN 24
HOURS.

CUSTOMER WENT TO STORE TO PICK
UP TWO-PIECE EQUIPMENT. UPON
UNPACKING DISCOVERED ONE PART
NOT PART OF THE UNIT.

DECEMBER 21 CATALOG DEPARTMENT
CALLED TO ADVISE CUSTOMER OF
DELIVERY IN "FIRST WEEK OF JAN-
UARY"

DELIVERY!

DECEMBER 29

COMMUNICATION
*

tive for State Farm wrote the victim, "Although the arbitration committee found for the applicant in this case, we do not agree with its findings and must therefore respectfully decline any voluntary payment."

The victimized driver then wrote to the president of State Farm Insurance Company. His letter was referred to the company's regional vice president. The regional vice president responded by letter. He wrote, "Certainly a personal conference to discuss the merits of our respective positions would be most appropriate." A meeting with the "divisional claim superintendent" was suggested.

Since the offending Car B was covered by another insurance company with headquarters in San Antonio, Texas, the victim once again contacted Crawford and Company (with national headquarters in Atlanta, Georgia), the company handling the case as adjuster. More delay and more artistic shuffling.[2] Five days before the first anniversary of the accident, the matter was taken out of orbit when a check was delivered to the innocent victim.

The artistry of decision postponement by twiddlisms in series has been mastered by the insurance industry. Such mastery should serve as an inspiration to dedicated finger tappers throughout the world. There are few instances in the annals of governmental bureaucracy in which such simple decisions have been postponed so skillfully.[3]

The taxpayers of America have contributed billions of dollars to support the fine art of nonresponsive twiddling, but the insurance industry has extracted even more money from the ranks of its policyholders and the victims of its insured. Nonresponsiveness at its best.

Governmental bureaucrats are timid finger tappers when compared to their insurance-industry counterparts. They can do better!

[2]A taxi driver in a similar accident in Memphis, Tennessee, observed insurance-industry twiddlisms for more than two years before settlement was made. Exciting inaction!

[3]The Municipal Council of Dorchester, England, is a local unit of government that excelled in the orbital-referral technique. Eighteen years after being petitioned to build a small baby-carriage ramp over a curb in front of a city-owned cottage, the workmen arrived to build the ramp. The "baby" for whom the ramp was to be built was celebrating her engagement to be married when the spokesman for the municipal council explained that the ramp was a low-priority project.

10

A Bureaucratic Plan for Full Employment

SIMPLIFIED DIAGRAM OF STUDY COMMISSIONS IN
EARLY STAGE OF ORGANIZATIONAL PROLIFERATION

ith apparent motivation from the highest levels of government, a new and imaginative mechanism has been developed to reduce the rate of unemployment to be reported to the people of the nation. There are two basic approaches to affecting the published rate of unemployment: (1) Put more people to work, and (2) restructure the statistical analysis of unemployment data.

Authoritative sources in Washington have reported that high government officials responded with ecstasy when a middle-level bureaucrat in the Bureau of Labor Statistics verified to senior officials that administrative analysis of unemployment statistics offered a viable means of goal-oriented reporting. His study was based on the rediscovery of a basic mathematic principle. By altering the value of the numerator or the denominator of a given fraction, the value of the fraction can be altered. Thus, by merely changing the informational inputs into either the numerator or the denominator of categorized data, the Bureau of Labor Statistics can demonstrate dramatic or semi-dramatic—as warranted by the occasion—changes in the unemployment rate of the nation. While more people may be unemployed or underemployed, the rate can be adjustively computed to indicate to voting citizens whatever unemployment information high government officials believe they should hear.

While most professional bureaucrats can readily appreciate the adjustive methods of statistical computation, there have been some who have failed to understand that statistical integrity, like rhetorical integrity, must be adaptable. To a probu, statistical projections are means to accomplish an end rather than ends in themselves. It has been reported by informed sources in Washington that some purists in the Bureau of Labor Statistics have had difficulty understanding that statistics are to be used as national-policy instruments rather than for analytical and reporting purposes. Some of the purists found opportunities to change the direction of their career ladders, and those who are still with the bureau have chosen to cautiously residuate.

The probuistic plan for full employment is based on the principles of organizational proliferation, and it reflects effective utilization of bureaucratic counterpointing.[1] Since the primary instrument of public policy today is the study committee, the probuistic plan would build upon that solid foundation.

Washington tradition demands that where boards and commissions function, there will be a natural unfolding of sub-boards and sub-commissions. The first step toward implementation of the probuistic plan, therefore, will be to accelerate the ultimate proliferation pattern of Phase I and Phase II. Under the parentage of the Wage Board and the Price Commission, a series of new entities should be established.

Specifically, a Presidential Study Commission (PSC) should be appointed in each country of each state of the union. The commissions would be charged with the responsibility of studying local factors affecting the local economy. To assist the Presidential Study Commissions in their pondering of the multiphase factors a liaison office should be established in the White House. The White House Unemployment Liaison Office (WHULO) would help devise the questionnaires with which the country-level commissions could seek the counsel and recommendations of the country's citizens. Ultimate decision on the questionnaire, of course, would rest with a coordinating office to be established in the office of the Secretary of Labor. The membership of the country-wide Presidential Study Commissions will be determined by the President, acting upon the recommendation of the Secretary of Labor.

A series of Blue Ribbon Review Commissions (BRRC), not to

---

[1]The term "probuistic" is used to denote purposeful bureaucratic planning or other functional service by *professional* bureaucrats. It differs from the term "bureaucratic" in that bureaucratic artistry, though beautiful in execution, may be accidental in process and nondirective in purpose. That which is bureaucratic may be as beautiful as that which is probuistic, but probuisms can be developed only by the professional practitioners of the bureaucratic art. A child may pull a tooth but only a dentist may professionally extract. To a probu, it is not the result but the process that is important.

exceed one hundred in each state, should be established under the direction of the White House. For selecting members of the Blue Ribbon Review Commissions, the President may wish to establish a Blue Ribbon Review Commission Advisory Board (BRRCAB) to make specific recommendations on broad policy and commission membership. The BRRC's would review, within guidelines established by the White House Unemployment Liaison Office, the reports of the Presidential Study Commissions.

There should be an appropriate instrumentality to coordinate the various study efforts in each state, and for this purpose, each state should be divided into study regions. Each state should have from three to five State Survey Commissions (SSC), the final number to be decided by the respective state legislatures with the concurrence of the White House Unemployment Liaison Office. The survey commissions would study the reports of the studies made by the Blue Ribbon Review Commissions of the reports of studies made by the Presidential Study Commissions.

With regional boundaries to be established by the Congress, the probuistic plan includes a provision for the nation to be divided into nine regional organizations known as Regional Coordination of Studies, Reviews, and Surveys (RCSRS). The jurisdictional boundaries of the nine regional offices would be determined by the National Security Council upon the recommendation of the Cabinet.

The probuistic plan for full employment would thus be a natural projection from the excellent beginning made by Phase I and Phase II. Under the label of Orbital Phase III, the plan can be summarized as being one in which several thousand PSC's would collaborate with the WHULO in developing reports for review by the BRRC with advice from the BRRCAB, which in turn would submit reports to the SSC's for coordination of the reports of study recommendations to the RCSRS's for scrutiny and review before being submitted to the CLC/RE.

When the complete network of commissions is operational, the President could summarily instruct the members of the commissions to be innovative in their approach to economic stabilization. It is through committees, of course, that creativity, within established guidelines, can best be implemented.

By the projections from Phase I and Phase II, and by the optimized utilization of the study-committee mechanism, *the unemployed of the nation can be put to work studying the unemployment problem!*

3

Career
Programming
for Promotion
and Survival

Potentis
Reposit
Obscurantum

AVOID BEING THE BEARER OF ILL TIDINGS.

IF THE REORGANIZATION GOES THROUGH,
YOU MAY LOSE YOUR PARKING SPACE

here are men and women who counsel young executives, beginning teachers, or newcomers to public service that they should not "rock the boat" or become "involved" in matters controversial. Others counsel the beginning bureaucrats that "out of sight, out of mind" is the pathway to organizational success. Certainly this is not the counsel that reflects credit upon the great heartbeat of creative bureaucracy!

Inspiring leaders who have helped develop the state of the bureaucratic art to its present level of enriched institutionalization counsel the bureaucratic trainee in other terms. The typical message might be: "Ask not those questions and partake not of the the fruit that may alter the balance of the ship of state but stand firmly as an anonymous team member who is ready to sacrifice personal gain and recognition in the best interest of the organization."

In keeping with the counsel of the masters of the bureaucratic art, the trainee or junior member of a business organization should place his future in the hands of the corporate managers who serve as the head of the operating team. The young public servant should have faith in his agency's personnel system and devote his full time and energies to submerging self and possible disrupting ideas in the great drama of policy implementation. The young teacher or professor should devote his full being to the classroom and the mastery of his field. The direction of the educational endeavor and the intellectual pursuit of truth are matters best left in the hands of the head of the team!

FOLLOWING SUPERVISORY LEADERSHIP

In the long run, bureaucrats will find organizational accreditation through following the wise counsel of the supervisory leadership. The rare occasions of his departmental surfacing should serve as a simple indication that he wishes to be a member of the team. He should testify by both action and inaction his belief in the principles of executive orchestration and interface avoidance. This identification can be strengthened by discreetly volunteering for duties that do not fall within his prime responsibility with the organization.

The wife of the department head or executive vice president, for example, may seek a cheerful and convincing Santa Claus to assist in her favorite charity's Christmas-time program. The vice principal may unexpectedly find that he needs an additional chaperone for a weekend educational tour of a national forest. The dean may determine that he needs truly high-level volunteer tutoring for the sincere but underachieving son or daughter of a member of the board of trustees. A young foreign-service officer may accomodate the ambassador (and thus the country team) by guiding the wife of a VIP on a day-long shopping tour for "the things to buy here." These are the small but important opportunities for the young bureaucrat to adroitly but only occasionally surface for that quiet proof of his reverent responsiveness to the "good of the team."

There is a fine but treacherous line that divides the successful volunteer from the bronze-billed sparrow species whose fringeful but constant hovering about the executive feeder or watering hole becomes counterproductive. Minimal presence and faithful willingness conform to the best identity goals of the bureaucrat.

BEAR NO ILL TIDINGS

Trainees should avoid being placed in the position of serving as the bearer of ill tidings. The misfortune of being sent to seek the return of a superior from the golf course is matched only by the role of the emissary who must intrude upon a board meeting to quietly inform his administrative chief that an accusing pregnant lady awaits him in the anteroom. Legislative rejection of educational appropriations, sudden declines in the market, ousting of administrators, cancellation of international-travel orders, loss of parking privileges—these are but illustrative of the substantive messages the bureaucrat should avoid communicating to superiors if any remedial option can be devised. Such a communicative role firmly establishes a negative employee identity. Successful practitioners of the art are never caught in such a crisis-oriented position.[1]

With these suggestions concerning rare and cautious employee surfacing, the bureaucrat also is admonished to lose himself in his work and bloviate in the stimulating task of fostering the creative *status quo*.[2] By concentrating on his area of assignment and by caponizing his urges for direct action, he may acquire the status of constructive anonymity that is characterized by strength of security.

Political bureaucrats are particularly careful about the type of information that goes forth from their offices. When a new public-works program has been approved in a congressman's district, for example, he quickly translates the advisory information provided him by the government agency into appropriate press-release terms. "Congressman _____ announced today. . . ." When a veterans' hospital or military base is being closed, however, the congressman residuates until the government agency makes the announcement. He then blasts the executive branch for the decision. No member of the Congress will ever be the bearer of ill tidings.

AVOID NEGATIVE MIND-FIX

At the period of annual promotion, the decision-maker or rater will tend to accept recommendations readily when he has no negative mind-fix on the bureaucrat. In the matter of written evaluations, it is easier for the superiors to accept and extol than to reject and criticize. Rejection and negative ratings (1) must be justified in great detail thus requiring the senior bureaucrat to devote much time to writing a report he will have to defend; (2) may result in hearings on employee appeals; (3) ultimately must be the subject of uncom-

---

[1]Some successful practitioners not only seek to avoid being the messenger of ill tidings, but they also busily engage themselves in some activity of great importance until the post-crisis plateau has been reached. Such standard but impregnable activities are: emergency sick leave, culmination of negotiation for an alumni gift to the educational institution, wrap-up session on a major sale, conference with a prospective client, and drafting a response to a priority White House request. Some probus are noted for their creativity in developing activities for immediate crisis dropout.
[2]Bloviation was developed to its highest point as a basking art by President Warren Harding. He used the term to describe his stimulating and inactive visits to the rural areas of the nation.

fortable discussion with the junior colleague; and (4) may tend to reflect negatively on the employee development leadership of the senior bureaucrat who, in turn, will be rated by some superior tribunal.

Many professional bureaucrats place a note or "tickler" on their calendar to remind them of the evaluation guidelines some six to eight weeks before the performance ratings or promotion recommendations are to be written. During the finalization period, they can unobtrusively signal their outstanding performance in each of the performance factors.

The art of unobtrusive signaling combines the highest skills of the professional bureaucrat into an orchestrated pattern of cautious perceptibility. Inconspicuous surfacing at moments when the supervisor is happy should be combined with subliminal projection of positive rating factors. The beginning bureaucrat should avoid the practice of unobtrusive signaling, however, until he has had an opportunity to test the level of his artistry in his church, fraternal, and civic organizations. Only after he has attained the level of the successful practitioner, should he utilize the art form in his professional life. When in doubt about his signaling skill, he should obscurate.

Potentis reposit obscurantum! In obscurity lies strength.

12

Filing for
Future Fidelity

CREATING THE VINTAGE MEMO

y whatever interpretive system he uses, the bureaucrat should present information in an orbital context. He should use qualifiers and adjustive abstractions in communications in order that future interpretation can fit the most advantageous policy position at the moment in question.

One mark of the professional bureaucrat is his ability to draw from his files an early vintage memorandum that will reflect the sagacity and wisdom of his recommendations. It is absolutely essential, therefore, that the bureaucrat keep a *personal* file of his memoranda. Organizations rarely have a "memory bank" due to the constant change of personnel. This gives the professional bureaucrat an important resource-intensive advantage.

Amateurs in the bureaucratic scene have been concerned that computers may endanger their use of intuitively autistic memos. Probus, however, have indicated no great concern about computerization in this regard, for they are confident that their skill in the use of qualifiers and adjustive abstractions will surpass the skills necessary for programming of their memoranda. As computers speed the processing, the probus merely add new sets of channels and infuse more variables in the parameters of the problems being programmed.

SELECTING VINTAGE MEMOS

Frequent changes in corporate management, educational administrators, and government officials result in many opportunities for probus to make effective use of carefully selected vintage memos. Sound bureaucratic forecasting must provide for optional interpretations that will assure the forecaster's sequential wisdom.

A corporate official, for example, might write the following memoranda with one being sent to each of two corporate officials in separate divisions; or, one memo to an official and one "for the files." The drafting date may be separated by a few days.

Memo A

In viewing the configurative presentation by the representatives of the Vago complex, it would seem that the merger proposal should be subjected to the most careful analysis that the state of the art will permit. Specifically, the dominance factors must be carefully correlated to the variable market fluctuations with a trajectory time phase that would permit an acceptable level of threshold activity. If the total correlation is not in a harmonious relationship with the qualitative and quantitative management thrusts, I would suggest that the decision on the merger be postponed . . . or possibly even rejected. This is too serious a matter to justify hasty action, and I strongly counsel careful study of the factors outlined above.

Memo B

Assuming that the precommital factors have been weighed against the restructured quantitization, and assuming that the merger can be effected within the present market coordinate, it is my opinion that the restructured residuals within established parameters would indicate that favorable action be taken on the merger proposal. The critical variable is that of time, and I recommend, within the bounds outlined above, that the merger possibility be pursued with diligence.

Having placed a double set of clear carbons of the two memos in his personal file, the professional bureaucrat can peruse the maturing scene before him and relax in the anticipatory knowledge that, regardless of the decision or the results thereof, he will be proven to be an authoritative strategist on corporate acquisitions.

ANTIMEMO?

Stop writing memos? A low-key campaign?
Be this your counsel, my lord, to halt the matters of state by banish-
    ing the employment of paper?
Darest thou change the habits of the ages and remove honour from
    those who serve the kingdom?
Woe upon ye, and all such men of decision and office who would
    bring change in the name of progress. . . .
Nay who would bring revolution under the false banner of the vir-
    tuous fight!
May the Civil Service Commission defend us!
But, hold, my noble lord! For memory sings that 'tis the season for
    such protests,
And it is a custom more honour'd in the breach than the observance.
Methinks I shall entreat to patience the soldiers of Noble Probu,
For knoweth they in their hearts that ours is an eternal and noble
    isle protected round about by a sea of bubbling glue.
*O prudent bureaucracy! Thy cannons shall have their bowels full
    of paper,*
*And ready mounted are they to split forth their rain of memos that
    thou shalt stand as sovereign and vanquisher.*

Preservation
of the Species

DECISION-MAKING POSITION WITH
A VEGETABLE MARKETING UNIT

he recruitment and initiation of budding bureaucrats are obligations that each probu must accept with heart and mind if the cause of the *status quo* is to be served. Identification of potential recruits is often effected through observation of families already within the bureaucratic orbit. Sons and daughters, cousins and aunts, sisters and uncle—all relatives of practicing probus make prime candidates for filling personnel "slots" that may become available through arranged transfers, retirements, or the creation of new positions.

By recruiting relatives of practicing bureaucrats, the probu can help weave the web of institutional security that is a goal of the bureaucratic brotherhood. Of course, no probu would dare to place a relative in his or her own bureau, but would utilize one aspect of the well-recognized "buddy system" through which a bureaucratic colleague places the relative in his bureau. The "buddy" thus earns a callable credit for future contingencies.[1]

[1]For example, Jonathan Harley, an official with the Department of the Army, wished to place his sister-in-law in a secretarial position in the Federal Trade Commission. A member of his car pool, James Nelson, was a senior-level probu who had recently transferred from FTC to the Pentagon. Nelson was successful in guiding his friend's sister-in-law into the position. One callable credit earned. When a new appointee sought to abolish Nelson's position in the department, he called on Harley, who managed to save the position. Callable credit called; *status quo* maintained. Though the caliber-credit system permeates the governmental bureaucracy and functions well without familial ties, the recruitment of

While dedicated and reverent response from the developing bureaucrat is essential for acceptance into the operational sphere of dynamic inaction, it is the probu who must provide the inspirational and instructional dialogue with the bureaucratic aspirant.

Under the guidance of the probu, the budding bureaucrat should not merely gather together application forms and begin to fill in the blanks, but he should develop with care an inventory of his past accomplishments. All paying and nonpaying work experience should be listed. The inventory should include summer and part-time jobs held during student days, and it should include volunteer activities with church, fraternal, and other organizations. The list should be pondered, revised, and matured for several days before the first word is written on an application form. Such guidance from the probu will help the budding bureaucrat distinguish himself from the mere job-seeker.

Assume, for example, that a young man has an experience profile that includes these elements:

1. As a student in high school, he worked in a grocery store with the prime responsibility for removing rotten tomatoes, lettuce, and other vegetables from the display shelves.
2. For one summer, he typed and assembled briefs and other papers prepared by a law student working in a one-man law firm.
3. As a university student, the aspirant worked at a neighborhood swimming pool teaching boys and girls to swim.
4. He served as a marshal in four protest demonstrations.

Assume also that the young man has pondered with great care the employment goals that shall guide his life, and he has determined that he wishes a position with one of four organizations. The four: International Telephone and Telegraph (ITT), Inter-American Development Bank, Harpers Ferry High School (teaching position), and the Department of the Army.

The budding bureaucrat should make a careful evaluation of the philosophical and operational thrust of the four organizations. Armed with this information *and* the experience profile, he can develop a work chart that recasts or translates his qualification into those terms most appropriate for each organization. Organogram Number Four D/Delta illustrates the interpretive approach.

---

one's relatives or the relatives of other probus helps assure a commonality of interest and an avoidance of disturbing interfacing.

Aspiring Bureaucrat's Experience Profile

Prospective Employer	Sorting Rotten Vegetables	Typing for Student Briefer	Teaching Exchange Students How to Swim	Marshal in Protest Demonstrations
International Telephone and Telegraph	Decision-making position in a vegetable marketing unit. Experienced in shredding rejects.	Assistant to chief briefer in a law firm. Coordinated security plans relating to internal documents.	In charge of a small but important educational program with direct supervision of fifteen trainees; emphasis on international programs.	Official position to moderate shareholders'' demands for change in management. Experienced in evading confrontation with domestic authorities.
Inter-American Development Bank	Variable grading of vegetables with emphasis on marketing factors.	Document preparation for use in policy determination.	Directed a technical assistance program with a focus on transference of skills.	Served as an adviser in fostering self-help efforts in the implementation of an international program with emphasis on local initiative.
Harpers Ferry High School (teaching position)	Worked on motivational consumer factors in a community-oriented enterprise.	Assisted in studies concerning the individual's relationship to community standards as reflected in local ordinances and state/national statutes.	In charge of a youth instructional activity with emphasis on individual needs and performance standards.	Motivational supervisor in a mass program designed to alter national goals and targets.
Department of the Army	Established parameters on product differentiation and implemented quality control program on specified food products.	Directly responsible for preparation of specialized documents that served as basis for strategic planning and action.	Planned and executed a program designed to meet student performance objectives of increased mobility in aquatic elements.	Key position in an organized effort to prevent unauthorized incursion and to foster self-discipline and prudence in a highly motivated and articulate group of citizens.

NOTE: The budding bureaucrat must learn to translate his work experience into those terms that are compatible with the philosophical and operational thrust of the organization with which he seeks employment.

If the budding bureaucrat encounters any translation problem, he should feel free to request assistance from some practitioner of the bureaucratic art whom he may know. He should prepare a "piece of paper" or draft of his translation efforts before calling on the practitioner for help. The first drafts of memos, position papers, "think pieces," program proposals, and other standard works of bureaucracy are written at the lower level. The middle- or senior-level professional bureaucrats are the "clearance" specialists who are skilled in the use of the blue line, the marginal question mark, and scissors and paste. Without a draft of an application translation in hand, the budding bureaucrat may disturb the established thought patterns of the practitioner and create a temporary frustration "spin-out" that may affect "the harmonics of the linear relationship."

The aspiring bureaucrat should make a ponderable review of those notes to establish whom he knows who knows some official, stockholder, political contributor, trustee, or other "keeper of the keys" that may be called upon for a favorably honest as well as imperative type recommendation. Their names should be listed as references in the application form with appropriate emphasis on those reference resources applicable to the organization approached in each application. Some professional bureaucrats suggest listing only one "power contact" in the application, thus preserving the other such contacts for what is professionally known as "the big push."

Sensitivity to functional criteria of institutions and/or personnel officers is helpful in initial placement. The probu is obligated to assist in the growth of his bureacracy and to the preservation of the species. There is no finer way to fulfill this obligation than to participate in the recruitment and placement of potential bureaucrats.

Machiavelli,
the Failure

hough ultimately a failure, Niccolo Machiavelli has provided *some* inspiration and helpful guidance to political bureaucrats (polibus) and administrative bureaucrats (adminibus) in his classic work, *The Prince.* The personal philosophy of Machiavelli is a subject worthy of continuing study by a committee of scholars because there are questions yet to be pondered concerning his role as observer and his role as practitioner. The incontrovertible fact, however, is that Machiavelli was a bureaucrat at heart.

In the cover letter accompanying his nonremunerative consultative report to Prince Lorenzo, Machiavelli reflected his adherence to the rules of the successful ponderer. "With the utmost diligence," he wrote, "I have long pondered and scrutinised the actions of the great, and now I offer. . . ."[1] In his advice to the prince, Machiavelli wrote:

> I also believe that he is happy whose mode of procedure accords with the needs of the times, and similarly he is unfortunate whose mode of procedure is opposed to the times. For one sees that men in those things which lead them to the aim that each one has in view, namely, glory and riches, proceed in various ways; one with *circumspection,* another with *impetuosity,* one by *violence,* another by *cunning,* one with *patience,* another with *the reverse,* and each by these diverse ways may arrive at his aim.[2]

In spite of being a failure, Machiavelli

[1]Niccolò Machiavelli, *The Prince* (New York: New American Library, 1952), p. 31.
[2]*Ibid.,* p. 121.

has thus provided a degree of insight into the practical patterns of governmental life that: (1) citizens may find his words helpful in understanding how bureaucrats function, and (2) bureaucrats may learn how to move upward and onward within bureaucracies.

CIRCUMSPECTION

Though few in number, there have been recorded instances in which bureaucrats have been promoted by being circumspect and available. An academic bureaucrat, for example, wished to move from a professorship to a deanship. He observed that his dean was reaching the retirement age, and he also observed that the institution's president highly valued the dean's recommendations. The professor developed a plan by which he would volunteer in a cautious manner to assist the dean with some of the tedious and unglamorous work of the dean's office. The professor helped draft reports for the college, accepted off-hour assignments on study committees, and wrote departmental budgets. He demonstrated unquestioned loyalty to the dean and president in faculty meetings.

The cautious but fringeful hovering about the nest of the decision-makers brought him ultimately to the deanship. The circumspect campaign was low key, and was based on evident loyalty and ready availability. And, being a *known* quality, he was not considered likely to disrupt the ongoing plans of the president. In making his recommendation, the dean was not unmindful of the probability that his successor would tend to preserve the past program and thus provide his "mentor" with institutional immortality.

IMPETUOSITY

Impetuous action is not consistent with the accepted *modus operandi* of the professional bureaucrat. Though temporary gains can be made by what Machiavelli labeled as "impetuousity," long-range career goals are better served by the soothing pattern of inaction. Excessive brass may be as disruptive in bureaucratic interfacing as it is in a woodwind quartet.

VIOLENCE

Direct eradication of a superior who stands as a barrier to a bureaucrat's promotion is not recommended. Nor is the secondary use of a removal contract in keeping with the bureaucrat's inherent regard for minimal risks. Not only is violence a potentially embarrassing way to clear the underbrush for a promotion but it is also an elementary and unprofessional technique. The state of the art has developed to the point that a professional bureaucrat has available to him a wide range of sophisticated maneuvers that are in keeping with his professional status. Sophistication and artistry are always preferred to simplicity and unskilled execution.

CUNNING

Machiavelli, though a failure when measured by the bureaucrat's ultimate test, was on target when he paid tribute to cunningness as an important characteristic of those who gain and retain power. The cunning bureaucrat, like the articulate mumbler, is only limited in the development of his skill by the confining barriers to creativity that he himself builds.

A bureaucrat, for example, may assist his superior in developing an important proposal that will be presented to the organization's administrator. He raises no questions and, indeed, he gives encouragement to his superior, even though he has learned from the administrator's secretary during an evening conference that the administrator wants a proposal totally different from the one being developed. During the formal presentation of the proposal to the administrator, the bureaucrat eagerly watches for an opportunity to make an effective thrust that may surprise and shock his superior but will find warm concurrence from the administrator.

The thrust must be made in the tones of deep concern, but the message must be one that shows the challenger's quickness of mind as well as soundness of judgment. For example, he might say to his superior, "George, I know you have been working long and hard on this proposal, but listening to your presentation, it occurs to me that. . . ." *Thrust Number One of a cunning bureaucrat!*

The cunning bureaucrat knows, however, that he must time his thrusts so that they occur shortly *after* efficiency ratings have been made, thereby giving him a full year to complete the replacement of his superior. He also recognizes that Thrust One must be followed immediately by Thrust Two and Thrust Three. This involves setting up his target again and again.

One effective setup is to generate questions to the administrator that deal with the immediate superior's area of expertise. The questions should be posed by a congressman, if possible, and should deal with a highly controversial and emotionally loaded issue. If the organization deals with health matters, the question can request a policy position on abortion or on distribution of birth-control devices to sixteen-year-old girls. If the organization deals with educational problems, a firm policy position may be requested on school bussing.

The bureaucrat should try to stimulate a question that will evoke a response from his superior that will trigger a violent reaction from the congressman. The congressman might call the administrator to testify on the policy statement before a congressional committee. Most administrators are uncomfortable about testifying before committees because questions and comments may escalate into more problems. When the administrator demands to know who was responsible for him being called before the congressional committee, he will be given the name of the "problem-making" superior. *Thrust Two.*

The bureaucrat can arrange other setups in which minor but embarrassing questions can be indirectly fed to industry leaders or representatives of the press. If the superior's name appears in the press as the person responding to a "can't win" question, the bureaucrat will have made another important mark. Or, if a newspaper quotes the superior but identifies him only as "an informed source," the administrator will demand to know the name of the person speaking to the press without prior clearance. *Thrust Three.*

If the bureaucrat has a proper working relationship with an industrial or professional group whose interests are opposite to those of the agency's policy, the superior can be invited to attend the group's national convention. If the convention is to be held in Puerto Rico, Honolulu, or other interesting location, it is probable that the superior would accept the invitation quietly instigated by the bureaucrat. The superior's presence at the "policy session" can be requested after he is in attendance at the convention. Without prior notice, the superior can be invited to defend the agency's policy before the antagonistic participants in the convention's plenary session. If he declines, he loses; if he responds, he loses. If the press is present, he may win. More headlines. Regardless of what happens, he cannot win. *Thrust Four.*

The bureaucrat who is cunning and patient will ultimately bubble to the top.

PATIENCE AND THE REVERSE

Patience is a quality that the professional bureaucrat must develop, but a promotion that comes merely from waiting is a promotion that often comes too late to permit the bureaucrat to enjoy the full fruits of a senior position. Patience is therefore a quality and not a technique. Similarly, the reverse of patience is not a genuine operating technique. Impatience, of course, can result in premature thrusts and endanger the promotion-oriented enterprise. Impatience may thus lead the bureaucrat to disaster but certainly Machiavelli was somewhat unprofessional when he indicated that patience is one of "those things which lead" princes (or, one could say, bureaucrats) to the achievement of their goals. Though patience is in keeping with the principles of dynamic inaction, it is not operationally sound as a guideline for the bureaucrat who is seeking the techniques that will win him a promotion.

MACHIAVELLI'S FAILURE

A successful bureaucrat can always equate personal ambition and bureaucratic survival with the good of his organization. Indeed, duty demands it! In his quest for techniques that will gain promotions and assure survival, the professional bureaucrat can learn much from Machiavelli, but he should remember that the Florentine strategist wrote his advisory treatise while in exile. The tactition wrote from a base of failure.

Machiavelli, the noted fifteenth-century senior bureaucrat. made **many missions** to heads of state as the military- and foreign-affairs secretary for the Republic of Florence. After thirteen years of successful public service, however, he did not meet the basic standard by which all professional bureaucrats are judged.

The ultimate test of bureaucratic competency is the test of survival. It was in the survival test that Machiavelli failed. Despite his thirteen years of service, and despite the senior level already attained by him, Machiavelli was unable to survive the change of administration when the Medici returned to power. Exile was the penalty for bureaucratic failure.

Niccolo Machiavelli failed to survive. Niccolò Machiavelli was a failure.

Vertical and Lateral Placement

ESTABLISH IDENTITY WITH THE RECEPTIONIST

robus as well as budding bureaucrats should be alert to opportunities to move from bureau to bureau or department to department within a single organization. Many probus have employed the transfer technique as a vehicle for promotion. If the transfer does not involve an immediate "increase in grade," a lateral (same grade) transfer may involve a promise of a promotion. The key to upward in-house movement is knowledge of the number of "slots" or positions that are available at various grade levels in various offices.

A budding bureaucrat seeking his first job or a probu seeking a transfer may find it advantageous to have high-level assistance in obtaining the appointment for a placement interview. The fine line between skillful and fumblistic arrangements, however, is one that must be studied carefully. An error in the use of high-level resources can result in negative echo that can complicate the aspirant's placement in the bureaucratic state.

CONGRESSIONAL CONTACTS

If the bureaucrat desiring a particular governmental position has friends or relatives who have financially or otherwise contributed to the election of a member of Congress, he may seek a congressionally generated appointment for an interview. If the congressman or his administrative assistant merely contacts an agency's congressional liaison office with a routine request for the appointment, it may be translated by the agency interviewer as a courtesy contact or "do-what-you-can-within-normal-rules-and-procedures" request. Such a contact may indicate a certain level of potential problems to the interviewer, but it also gives him maximum option in the placement recommendation he must make.

On the other hand, if the congressional message indicates "great and continuing interest" in seeing that the bureaucrat's talents are not lost to public service, this translates into "this one I must have, so lean on it." In this instance, the interviewer's options are reduced as are those of the senior official who must make the final placement decision.

If the congressman's record of support for the program administered by the agency is a negative one, however, his support may do the aspirant more harm than good. The negative echo may be even louder if the congressman is of the administration's opposition party. On the other hand, if the congressman is a member of the committee (or better yet, a member of the subcommittee) that has jurisdiction over the agency, the detrimental factors may be largely offset.

Just as it is wise for the bureaucrat to check the variables involved in the governmental sphere, so also the aspirant in the corporate or academic world should inquire discreetly about the level of rapport that his high-level contact (stockholder, trustee, senior official, etc.) has with the employment decision-makers. If this corporate reference, for example, has recently lost or is currently involved in a proxy fight with management, it could be a marginal reference to use! Does the bureaucrat, his family, or his friends know a major buyer of the corporation's product? A supplier of some scarce commodity? A member of the Appropriations Committee or regulatory agency?

If the aspiring bureaucrat should have no lead to someone to assist him with the arrangements for the interview appointment, he must take the bureaucratic "step of last resort" and do it himself.

When he ultimately arrives for the interview, he should schedule himself with sufficient time to become acquainted with the receptionist or the appointment secretary. There is no greater friend that a bureaucrat can have than the person who controls the gateway to the chief. The interviewer will probably keep the applicant waiting, anyway, but he should give as much time and attention to the gateway controllers as to the interviewer himself. While waiting, the bureaucrat should seek or make opportunities to visit with the receptionist or appointment secretary, but he should not take more of her time than she is desirous of sharing.

When ushered into the presence of the interviewer, the bureaucrat should greet him with a firm handshake, a subserviently confident greeting, and then settle down to let the interviewer officiate. The *Bureaucrat's CRON-T* should serve as guidelines for the meeting, and at some point in the discussion, all CRON-T elements should be covered. The CRON-T elements are:

1. A desire to make a *C*areer decision.
2. A relation of that career decision to the *R*eason that you have applied to the interviewer's organization.
3. The necessary interest in beginning salary is overbalanced by a desire for a position with *O*pportunity for personal growth and service through employment with the organization.
4. A recognition that there exists a *N*eed for the interviewer's help and guidance through the organization's hiring process.
5. A dedication to the principles of *T*eam play and an assurance that responsibilities will be discharged in the manner prescribed by superiors.

Other similar factors can be woven into the discussion, but the governmental, corporate, or academic bureaucrat should always run the check list of the *Bureaucrat's CRON-T* when seeking a position with a new organization.

At the completion of the interview, the bureaucrat or aspirant should express, of course, his appreciation for the opportunity of meeting the interviewer and for his generous help and guidance. He then should mention casually that he is very grateful to Congressman X or Mr. Y for his suggestion that the help of the interviewer be sought. He can thus incidentally indicate that he will give a favorable report on the interview to the high-level contact.

If an evaluation of the interview indicates that the applicant has a fifty-fifty chance of obtaining a position, he should immediately ask the congressman or other contact to write a warm letter thanking the interviewer for the fine reception and helpful suggestions. The original copy of the letter should not be sent to the interviewer himself, but to his superior. In the case of a governmental agency, the congressman or business contact can request that his letter be placed in the personnel file of the interviewer. Carbon copy to the interviewer.[1]

After the letter and carbon copy have had time to be received, the contact or sponsor can make a friendly inquiry as to the status of the application.

[1]Complimentary letters in governmental personnel files are seen by the agency promotional panels at the time of the annual performance evaluation. Such letters are treasured by professional bureaucrats who work for governmental agencies.

With appropriate orchestration of application and interview factors, the bureaucrat should be successful in obtaining a desirable position. Once he has his "foot in the door," he can devote time and energy to developing the skills of the professional practitioner of the bureaucratic arts. And, once inside an organization, he can watch for and help stimulate opportunities for lateral and supernal entry to other positions.

Personal promotion, 'tis consummation devoutly to be wished.

Performance
Standards
and
The Peter Principle

s the bureaucrat moves through the system of his chosen bureaucracy, he should constantly strive to improve his skill in making simple things more complex, and to increase the range of his noncommittal mumbling and writing. He should seek opportunities to participate in orbital dialogues and should make daily use of the Ponderer's Practice Sheet. Regular practice in the privacy of home or car may result in mastery of the difficult art of marathon mumbling. Development activities should be programmed by the individual bureaucrat if he is to achieve the level of the true professional.

Periodically, the probu should evaluate the results of his practice. The goal of his efforts, of course, is to move up the career ladder of the profession. The highest level that most dedicated probus may achieve is that of the Senior Professional Bureaucrat (SPB). In the realm of governmental, corporate, and academic bureaucracy, only the most dedicated can earn the noble title of "Senior Professional Bureaucrat."

The Peter Principle describes not only a person's movement up a career ladder but also it describes one's lateral entry into new career channels. In every bureaucracy, as Dr. Peter clearly stated, employees tend to rise to their level of incompetence. A bureaucrat may be an excellent thrummer in small informal staff meetings, but when promoted to a level at which he must thrum before large formal staff meetings, his thrummistic skills may have been exceeded. A fine small-meeting thrummer may be a poor large-meeting thrummer.

The values of competence base lines

vary with the relative placement patterns as they relate to organizational or individual goals. Or, a bureaucrat may be judged competent by another bureaucrat but incompetent by a businessman; a businessman may be judged competent by another businessman but incompetent by a professional bureaucrat. Therefore, the multi-phasic application of The Peter Principle can serve as an effectively adjustive yardstick when harmonized by a skillful practitioner of the bureaucratic arts.

To be known as a Senior Professional Bureaucrat is to have attained the highest level of probuistic success! Organogram Nine B/Iota has been developed as a guide to be used by probus in a program of self-evaluation of performance. By charting the course of improvement each day, the probu will be encouraged to direct all energies and skills toward the ultimate career objective of being named The Peter Principle Bureaucrat of the Year.

THE LIFE CYCLE

The excitement was great every hour of each day as I sat at the bureau chief's knee, to be taught how to mumble the message of steadfast bureacracy. T'was a difficult task for my logical mind, but the chief taught me all that he knew about orbital prose, multinegative cues, and adjustive subliminal views. He instructed me first in decision postponement and to master the mumblistic art, then he moved me along to the techniques and skills of interpreting tables and charts.

I remember the days in the fall of the year when the chief, in his favorite chair, quietly gazed through the door with his caliper eyes at the eyes of the girls passing there. He would puff on his pipe every once in awhile, and would mumble as few others could, about boldness of irresolution and what should be done when one's misunderstood. He would talk of old rules and procedures, and how he'd developed the state of the art. He would mumble of interface patterns and of men with a *status quo* heart. He would speak of the friendly old guidelines, and his eyes would flash with delight as he taught me to obligate funds at the end of the fiscal-year flight.

As I mastered each step of the bureaucrat's art, he would smile and then call in the staff. "Now, I'll make a prediction for all to record, so take notes and then file them away. This young man will be Deputy Associate Assistant Co-Administrator someday." So, I studied my lessons and learned them quite well; I now speak in a

	Senior Professional Bureaucrat	Competent Professional Bureaucrat	Developing Bureaucrat	Beginning Bureaucrat	Very Little Hope
Skill in Oral Communication	Speaks in inseparable but resonant tones that reflect deep and authoritative concern. Uses wide range of facial expressions and hand gestures. Excellent posture and complete mastery of Roget's *Thesaurus:* Excellent marathon mumbler.	Speaks in inseparable tones with full rhetorical integrity. Outstanding vocabulary. Moderately effective in marathon mumbling.	Speaks in inseparable tones but working vocabulary includes only a few multi-syllable words.	Speaks in distinguishable tones and uses simple terms to express ideas. Is able to mumble an occasional string of modifiers.	Can be understood.
Skill in Written Communication	Writes with adjustive integrity; presents ideas with maximized deliberative options. Reflects skill in constructive emulation, buzzing, and application of the Thesauric Formula. Can operate memo retraction shredder	Writes with adjustive integrity, but projects nonresponsiveness with minimal options. Excellent buzzer.	Writes with meaningful disparity, but semantical infusions are capable of analysis.	Writes with enriched projections that can be understood with study.	Can be understood.
Quality of Work	Is able to translate new policy statements into harmonized programs of the creative *status quo.* Develops guidelines and establishes parameters for adaptive compatability. Outstanding in constructive issue avoidance and decision postponement.	Is able to guide new policies into the operational mold of the creative *status quo.* Outstanding in issue avoidance.	Effectively assists in guiding new policies into harmonized programs of the creative *status quo.*	Participates in institutionalizing new policies.	Executes policies.
Quantity of Work	Practices dynamic inactivism and authoritatively studies interpretative proposals before dissenting or giving qualified approval. A prodigious ponderer and forthright twiddler.	Militantly optimizes the creative *status quo* by orchestrating variable guidelines related to the decision process. Rarely gives unqualified	Encumbers interpretive proposals for constructive verification before giving clearances.	Programizes proposals for maximized coordination before clearing.	Clears in minimum time.

mumblistic way, I can mumble and shuffle and furrow my brow; I can quote the *Thesaurus* at will. I can obligate funds by the thirtieth of June, and can orchestrate studies with skill. I can rough out reports and the surveys of studies, and blue-ribbon study reviews. I can mumble in high tones in committees and boards, and give balance to conflicting views.

Well, the chief has retired now, but memories are clear as I sit in his favorite old chair. Now I teach the young folks what I've learned through the years of the bureaucrat's laissez faire. And I smile as I gaze through the fog of the years in a search for elusive old thoughts. "Now, what was it?" I ask as I grope through the haze. "What was it I wanted to say? Oh, yes, I remember." I speak with great pride. "I received final word just today. The personnel panel and agency head have both cleared me for quite a promotion. Next week, I will be the new Deputy Associate Assistant Co-Administrator in Charge of Orbital Motion."

Survival
in a Changing
Administration

DURING A CHANGE IN ADMINISTRATION,
KEEP A LOW PROFILE

GOVERNMENTAL

ecurity of employment is relatively assured in the governmental world due to various provisions of the civil-service laws. The relativity factor revolves around such simple matters as temporary or limited appointments, low seniority, and the "bumping rights" through which career employees can bump those who have fewer years of service. These and similar provisions provide flexibility for an incoming administration to make some political adjustment in the ranks of government employees.

While security of employment is therefore relatively assured, the vulnerability of positions of influence are open to maximized shopping by political applicants, party leaders, congressional staff assistants, and White House specialists in charge of placing responsive appointees.

A shopping guide to key positions, though this is not its official title, is issued at the beginning of each new administration as a limited edition (a committee print) by the Senate Post Office and Civil Service Committee. Carefully guarded and thoroughly studied by those seeking to work and those seeking to place, the shopping guide indicates the senior positions in all government departments and agencies that are not "protected" by the civil-service regulations. In effect, the guide lists prime targets, and indicates dates of availability, salary, and other information of interest to the political leaders who have been "given a mandate" by the people of the nation.

Even before the restricted publication

oi the shopping guide, and long before the inauguration of the new President, the old hands of the political game descend on Washington with expectancy in their eyes, determination in their stance, and a list of their contributions to political victory clutched in their hands.

At the time of the inauguration, however, thousands upon thousands upon thousands of newcomers to political activity join the old hands in cornering their senators and congressmen to seek their help in being appointed to some high position. The newcomers recall fondly and expectantly an early handshake of the now victorious candidate. They continue their targetless pursuit of a position of importance and prestige.

Of course, the old hands and the representatives of trade and professional organizations are already drafting the press releases to congratulate the new administration on their man's appointment. Senators and congressmen are in constant touch with the campaign's top political operatives at the lesser-known offices of the President-elect. There, they are shoulder to shoulder with the party's national committeemen, state party chairmen, and major fund raisers.

Such is the general environment when the professional bureaucrat is eagerly but quietly, almost frantically but stoically, trying to strengthen his own threads with party stalwarts of the new administration. It is at this point that the greatest survival skill of the probu must come into play.

SURVIVAL CHECK LIST/GOVERNMENTAL

The techniques utilized by probus in surviving the traumatic experiences that accompany a change in administration are as numerous and as varied as the numbers of probus themselves. The accompanying check list is presented, therefore, not as an all-inclusive set of guidelines, but as a list of proven techniques that may be adopted or modified to meet the survival demands of the probu.

1. Lower-level bureaucrats may safely residuate until they are able to learn who the new boss will be.[1] Higher-level bureaucrats are the prime targets of political operatives.

[1]"Residuate" is the bureaucratic term to indicate that process through which the probu develops as low a profile as possible. Residuate is the probu's verb form that relates low profile to the residuum, the last remaining particle.

2. If a high-level probu has private doubts that his party will remain in power, he should have laid the groundwork to convert his position to the category that is protected by civil-service coverage. Carefully orchestrated in advance, the probu may be able to survive a change of administration by conversion, but it may be necessary to accept a slightly lower grade when making the switch. The object of probus, however, is survival.[2]

3. If possible, the probu should obtain an assignment on a departmental transition committee. The transition committee or unit is under the direction of the *incoming* forces, and an opportunity to show ability, reasonableness, and dedication to the good of the department or agency may help the probu retain his position or perhaps become a part of the new team. Transition-committee members normally take care of transition-committee members.

4. The probu should make an inventory of contacts with the victorious party. The contacts should include friends and, if possible, friends who were politically active or made recorded contributions to the victor. Congressional contacts can be particularly helpful.

5. At every opportunity, the probu should use the years of experience, the knowledge of the specialty language, and other devices to reflect indispensable expertise. Probus who know the departmental regulations are in fine position. A distinguished leader of an operating foundation once stated, "If you cannot dazzle them with your brilliance, baffle them with something else."

6. During the period of changing administrations, the probu may find it expedient to develop his Form 171 in order to be able to present it to some personnel officer or senior official should he be given an unexpected opportunity for the assignment that he had been striving to obtain for months.

7. If the atmosphere is a negative one, the probu may wish to transfer to a field position in some area other than that in

---

[2]In some societies, changes of administration are accompanied by the recognition of postliminy. Postliminy is derived from Roman Law and is the right of any person who has suffered banishment or has been taken captive to assume his former civic privileges when the original state has been attained. A Democrat, however, who served as an Assistant Secretary under a Democratic administration, may not necessarily be returned to the Assistant Secretary level when an intervening Republican administration is defeated. Nevertheless, an implied touch of postliminy pervades the scene when changes in administration do occur, and former members of the Little Cabinet are given special accord.

which he now serves. By being out of sight, the probu may be forgotten. If the probu serves in the Washington headquarters, and if he cannot arrange a transfer to the field or to an international position, he should develop as low a profile as possible. When in changing administrations, the probu should residuate.

SURVIVING THE CORPORATE CHANGES

Changes of management in a major corporation or in a small business enterprise are accompanied by essentially the same employment and position threats that characterize the changes of administration in the Federal Government. The style may be more scalpelistic than saberistic, but the results are the same.

A new chief executive officer of a corporation wants to have his own team with him as he moves to keep the campaign pledges he made to the stockholders who were a party to his victory. Even in changes that accompany an orderly promotion within the company, a change is a change is a change. And bureaucrats in all fields of endeavor know that change brings only problems. The probu should develop his own check list of survival factors, but the suggestions presented may be helpful.

SURVIVAL CHECK LIST/CORPORATE

1. Develop an inventory of friends among the stockholders who supported the management change; and an inventory of friends of friends. Use it.
2. Research for little-known facts about the new chief executive officer and his chief aides—areas of personal interest, hobbies, theater, etc. Use them.
3. If a transition committee is to function, manage to become a member of the committee. If unable to become a working member, serve in some lesser staff position. The spirit of teamwork will be demonstrated, but, more important, ability and dedication to the well-being of the company will be evidenced.
4. If unable to serve in some capacity with a transition committee, the corporate probu should brush up on the latest terminology

and trends in his area of specialty. By using such terminology and by surrounding himself with all the accouterments of the professional, the probu may successfully project indispensable expertise.

5. Maintain a steady flow of paper through the *in* and *out* boxes. If the flow is not sufficient to present the appearance of a busy desk, the probu should generate a flow. He can write a series of individually typed form letters to customers and friends on some fringeful business matter, or he can send for catalogs and industry bulletins from addresses in industry magazines.

6. Increase the number of incoming telephone calls by routine inquiries. While others in the office are at lunch, the probu should initiate as many telephone calls as possible. Since the persons being called will probably be at lunch also, you can leave word for call-backs.

7. Develop a working paper on the way in which your responsibilities should be changed (improved!) to meet the changing structure of the company. The paper should be presented with great care and planning, but the manner of presentation should be quite casual.

8. Until the probu can grasp the trends of personnel and management policies, surfacing should be minimal. A basic rule to use when there is some question about the extent to which the probu should be seen and heard is, "When in doubt, residuate."

SURVIVAL IN ACADEME

Tenure in academe is somewhat similar to a career position in the civil service of the Federal Government, but the academic bureaucrat seeking tenure must devote more time to developing the to-be-tenured image than the Federal practitioner gives to gaining permanency of status. Survival in time of administrative change in the public schools is primarily a matter of tenure.

In order to gain tenure, the teacher who is new to a school system should devote a minimal time to classroom teaching and more time to the administrative and housekeeping chores that constitute the genuine yardstick of performance evaluation. The fine teacher, therefore, is the teacher who, for example, will volunteer to chaperone bus trips, collect tickets at sporting events, and submit reports on schedule.

Of all times to be considered by public-school teachers in their campaign to be placed on tenure, the most important are: (1) maintaining classroom discipline; (2) the timely submission of reports (attendance, grades, those required for Federal grants, and others); and (3) making no ripples in the classroom. Nonrippling is achieved by conservatively routine teaching, use of noncontroversial teaching materials, and avoidance of controversial issues in classroom discussions.

SURVIVAL CHECK LIST/ACADEMIC: PUBLIC SCHOOLS (TENURE-ORIENTED)

1. Develop a reputation for maintaining discipline in the classroom.
2. Submit all reports on schedule: class attendance; grades; questionnaires from educational and other organizations.
3. Volunteer to chaperone school dances, football- and basketball-game buses, and special field trips.
4. Volunteer to collect tickets at sporting events.
5. Volunteer for hall duty or noon duty on the school grounds.
6. Volunteer to serve on parent-student-teacher association committees.
7. Prepare an emergency lesson plan for use when supervisors or administration officials visit your classroom.
8. Attend all faculty meetings, faculty-club meetings, and faculty picnics.
9. Develop a special program for the Back-to-School Night.
10. Keep a pretty bulletin board.
11. Keep all venetian blinds at the same level.
12. Keep the floors of classroom clean, and erasers dusted.
13. Help monitor the halls between classes.
14. In California, teachers should develop class goals to avoid the stullistic lance relating to tenure.)

In institutions of higher education, tenure is still somewhat important, but the problems of professional survival are greater. A new college or university president, for example, may make drastic organizational changes in the academic senate, the liaison committees that coordinate with educational associations. He may also alter new educational programs, and the direction in which grants will be expended.

The changing of the guard, therefore, is important to every professor. The sanctity of his educational domain must be preserved against the dangers of departmental reorganization, and the adequate funding of his program of basic research is essential if he is to have the basis for publishing in his field. If a professor wishes to protect his budget, he can best do so by willingly waiving academic rights and academic freedom.

If the professor obtained the funding for his program by his own initiative, he should be willing to permit the new administration to recast some of the funding. Such action will prove to the new president or dean that the academic probu is a team player, and will put the good of the team above such minor matters as educational programming and scholarly pursuits.

If a controversy should develop over some minor infringement on academic freedom, the probu must exercise extreme caution. If he posits with the new administration, he will damage his professional image in the eyes of many of his colleagues on the faculty of the institution and in other institutions. If he should oppose infringements on academic freedom, he will be identified by the administration, board of trustees, and givers of grants as one whose judgment is too questionable to be trusted on other matters relating to promotion and occasional honors. The academic probu who finds himself in such a position should immediately follow the example of his governmental colleagues: When in doubt, residuate.

SURVIVAL CHECK LIST/ACADEMIC: HIGHER EDUCATION

1. Publish.
2. Obtain grants for educational programs, and volunteer to share a major portion of the funds with the administration for its use in whatever manner it deems best. The probu may then conduct some type of program with the smaller operating budget.
3. Attend all welcoming functions for the new administrator.
4. Avoid organizational issues. Adjust to all organizational changes unless they affect the probu directly.
5. Avoid philosophical issues; leave educational direction and the classroom guidelines to the administrators who know best *what* should be taught, *when* it should be taught, and *how* it should be taught. Academic freedom is too academic a subject to matter.

6. Avoid public association with students, faculty members, and townspeople who are in opposition to the new administration.
7. Avoid being on radio or television shows on which embarrassing questions could be asked.
8. When in change, residuate.

For probus who must cover the obstacle course of a changing administration for the first time, there is no great need to panic. Administrations may come and administrations may go, but creative bureaucracy continues on and on and on. Ripples may occur occasionally as new hatchet men are added to personnel offices, but also hatchet men come and hatchet men go.

For the probu who is experiencing the first change in either government, business, or academe, the basic rules for all to follow are quite simple: When in charge, ponder. When in trouble, delegate. When in doubt, mumble. *And when in change, residuate!*

Organizational Technology of the Professional Bureaucrat

18
Bureaucratic Counterpointing

LET YOURSELF GO WITH
BUREAUCRATIC COUNTERPOINTING

ounterpoint, in music, is the art of polyphonic composition in which one or more melodies are added to a basic melody. The art of bureaucratic counterpointing involves adding layers of additional personnel, procedures, and organizational units to a basic program. Procedural and organizational integrity are assured by the utilization of bureaucratic counterpointing.

The artistic expression of bureaucratic counterpointing is not evidenced in bombastic and haphazard rearrangements of organizational charts, nor is it to be enjoyed in merely rewriting rules and regulations. A bureaucratic counterpoint may be the quiet but lilting melody of happy insertions of little rules; at other times, it may be the majestic blast of trumpets heralding a new system of management coordination.

COUNTERPOINTING AID

The 1972 "Reform of the U.S. Economic Assistance Program" is an outstanding example of bureaucratic counterpointing.[1]

The full-note prelude to the 1972 Reform included: (1) a Presidentially appointed blue-ribbon commission to recommend a new approach to foreign assistance; (2) a series of internal Agency for International Development (AID) task

[1]Hannah, John A., "Memorandum for AID Employees," Agency for International Development, Washington, D.C., January 24, 1972. Containing: "Reform of the U.S. Economic Assistance Program."

forces and committees; and (3) the blunt delivery of a legislative proposal to an unconsulted Congress. Three years of full-note prelude gave way to the dramatic movement of twenty-nine pages, a cover letter, and three organizational charts.

"The Redirection of Program Operations and Organization," the objective of the reform, forthrightly called for "a more collaborative style of assistance" in which AID would become a monitor. Since a "major thrust" of the redirected program would be programs of population and humanitarian assistance, a new Bureau for Population and Humanitarian Assistance (BPHA) was placed into institutional gestation. Among its functions, the new bureau was to "bring together under central direction" overseas voluntary activities. Nothing is better designed for the inspiration of volunteers than for them to be coordinated with centralized bureaucratic counterpointing.

A population office in a Technical Assistance Bureau (TAB) was scheduled for transfer to BPHA and elevated to the level of an operating office with global authority on population. But, wait! *Counterpoint!* "Population staff may be seconded from the Population Office to the Regional Bureaus to help fill their liaison and review needs."[2] And, all new projects had to be approved by the Administrator's office in order to assure "conformity" with policy and feasibility.

The 1972 Reform package for the economic assistance program places emphasis on sector analysis. By developing sector strategies, the assistance officials could deal with broad sectors such as agriculture and education and avoid focusing attention on what one official referred to as "nasty old countries that take our boats." Under the plan, the regional bureaus would retain program loan and technical staff capacities, but a *new* Bureau for Program Services (BPS) would be created to assume *commodity procurement, contracting, engineering,* and management support services. *Counterpoint!* But, "to meet the concern of the Regional Bureaus for responsiveness and adequacy of service from centralized offices," the regional bureaus would "retain one or two persons to provide advice in bureau management and to provide liaison with central management offices." *Counterpoint!*

As mutually agreed between the regional bureaus and the Bureau for Program Services, a limited number of *commodity procurement officers, contracting officers,* and *engineers* would be detailed from the Bureau of Program Services *back* to the regional bureaus that had them before the reform. Completing the orbit results in . . . *Counterpoint!*

---

[2]*Ibid.,* p. 13.

Technical Assistance Bureau, Program and Policy Coordination Bureau (PPC), Administrator's Advisory Council, Project Approval Committee, Inter-Agency Development Loan Committee, Office of Evaluation, Budget Office, Office of the Controller, and other offices will fill out the body of the new AID (or whatever it ultimately may be renamed). The beauty of bureaucratic counterpoint will ultimately fly on "a major wing for *Program Support*" and "a second major wing for *Management Support*."

A matter of grave concern for probus, however, is the announced plan of AID to abolish the grand old manual orders that have served so well for so many years. Yet, dedicated bureaucrats must be willing to lose a few short-term skirmishes if the overall gain through bureaucratic counterpointing is significant. Professional bureaucrats can be consoled in the fact that, though the friendly old manual orders may one day disappear, they would be replaced by a series of "Policy Determinations" issued by the AID Administrator "together with specialized handbooks on supporting operations."

Ah, counterpoint, how lovely be thy theme.

Planning
a Conference
for Dynamic Inaction

CONFERENCE AGENDAS SHOULD BE PLANNED
TO INSURE DYNAMIC INACTION

ost conferences and conventions have no disruptive effect on the *status quo,* but dedicated probus can help assure bureaucratic serenity by becoming involved in conference planning. Planning for inaction, of course, should be wrapped in the terminology of the activists. By adopting the terminology of the activists, the probus can introduce the fuzzistic philosophical elements into the conference planning so as to orchestrate the grand old principles of dynamic inaction into the conference programming. A probu should never fear new terms; he should help *define* them so as to include in the definitions the great principles of yesteryear.

The importance of presentation technology has been recognized by various governmental agencies. The Employee Development Branch of the U. S. Department of Commerce, for example, offered a special "presentations workshop" exclusively to Department of Commerce employees.[1] The sixteen-hour program was entitled "The Professional Workshop," and was designed "to develop a deeply felt awareness of the human processes involved in achieving brief, accurate, and forceful verbal-visual presentations of materials with high technical content, and to develop skill in preparing and staging presentations for audiences of any size down to one."

As a part of the "professional eloquence" program, the probus were of-

[1]Raymond E. Atteberry, Chief, Employee Development Branch, Personnel Division, "Memorandum for all Divisions and Offices," December 29, 1970, Bureau of the Census, U. S. Department of Commerce.

fered a series of lectures on "presentation psychophysics" that described "some startling facts about drawing conclusions." Another segment of the workshop was designed to deal with "presentation morphology," which included a study of the characteristics of credible messages; use of flip charts and chalk boards; "storyboarding"; creation of "speaker conjunctions"; use of pointers and handouts; and what to do "before leaving your office" and "before leaving your hotel room."[2]

The professional eloquence workshop was described by a Department of Commerce official as being "superior in content and about right in terms of method and length for Commerce." What is good enough for Commerce should be good enough for the nation's other probus. Even though professional eloquence involves professional mumbling, the workshops sponsored by the Department of Commerce did not give appropriate attention to the principles of dynamic inaction.

Planning for dynamic inaction is such an accepted art that probus can normally limit their participation on the planning committee to a monitoring role. Occasionally, however, the probu must respond with cautious diligence when some newcomer to an organization may demand that the conference result in some action-oriented program. The following check list may be of help to developing bureaucrats.

PRELIMINARY PLANNING

What is the purpose of the conference? Who is to participate? Over whose signature will the invitations be issued? Who will serve as the conference chairman or co-chairmen? Where will the conference be held? What dispersed facilities are available for housing and meeting rooms? What equipment will be available (duplicating machines, mimeographs, tape recorders, translation, etc.)? What committees are necessary to develop the total agenda and appoint committee chairmen? These are but some of the preliminary planning factors that must be studied before other steps can be taken. Obviously, a committee must develop the purpose of the conference; another committee must determine the time and place of the conference; and a committee must determine who will be selected to chair

---

[2]Morphology is defined in *The American College Dictionary* as "the patterns of word formation in a particular language, including inflection, derivation, and composition."

each conference committee. Such preliminaries can require as much as six months of orchestrated delay; longer, if a probu is chairman of the planning committee.

THE AGENDA

Once the preliminary factors are in orbit, the planning committee should appoint an agenda committee. Working from the preliminary report on the *purpose* of the conference, the agenda committee should strive to organize the conference program in such a way as to include some minor reference to the purpose of the conference. To foster dynamic inaction, the agenda committee should develop a long agenda. The items that reflect an action orientation should be at the end of the agenda. With appropriate conference planning, the program may move so far behind schedule that the action items may never be reached.

Early on the agenda, those designing for inaction can include such thought-provoking and dialogue stimulating items as: (1) definition of terms; (2) identification of problems; (3) establishment of priorities; and (4) adoption of new by-laws. The latter is particularly effective for international voluntary organizations. With an occasional bureaucratic thrust at these four items, the probus seeking to optimize the *status quo* may be able to postpone other conference business until an hour late in the conference.

An important function of the agenda committee is scheduling the time for coffee breaks. If an activist is to be on the program, and such a compromise may be necessary from time to time, the agenda committee can reduce his disruptive influence by scheduling him for an afternoon session following the coffee break. The agenda and physical-arrangements committee can also collaborate on the location at which the coffee will be served. If served in a nearby room or on another floor in the building, maximized conference dropouts will reduce even more the effect of the unsettling ideas that an activist may raise during his presentation.

THE SPEAKERS' COMMITTEE

An immediate division of the speaker's committee into two subcommittees is usually appropriate. One subcommittee will determine the topics to be assigned to speakers, and the other subcommittee will select the conference speakers. If the speakers and topics selected independently by the two subcommittees do not mesh, another round of meetings will be required to reach some accord. If the speakers selected cannot accept the invitation to participate in the conference, more committee sessions can result. If one or more of the speakers give a tentative acceptance, a special round of sessions with the program-printing committee is assured when the deadline for printing is past due. The orbital functioning of the speaker's committee can reflect the type of bold irresolution that can serve as an inspiration to other probus working on the conference.

COMMITTEE ON DISCUSSION-GROUP CO-CHAIRMEN

To promote dynamic inaction, there are no factors that can exceed the cautious selection of discussion leaders. Where possible, co-chairmen should be selected who are: (1) incompatible professionally; (2) professors, bureau chiefs, or political leaders; (3) excellent readers of papers; and (4) unknowledgeable of the Robert's Rules of Order. By blending these four factors into the selection of co-chairmen, the committee can almost guarantee that dynamic inaction will be given its full measure of glory. Authorities in a particular field can tell the discussion participants the facts of life and thus avoid loss of time in needless discussion. Researchers can be encouraged to read their papers to discussion sessions, and co-chairmen with divergent views can assure that the listeners will hear both sides of issues.

THE ARRANGEMENTS COMMITTEE

If the speakers and the agenda committees do not assure 100 percent inaction, the arrangements committee can be helpful in a mop-up operation. Imaginative conference arrangers can let their experience be reflected in many exciting ways. This is one area in which innovation can be encouraged by the most ardent espousers of the *status quo*.

1. The larger discussion sessions should be scheduled as noted in the printed program, in small meeting rooms, and the small discussion groups should be scheduled in large rooms. If changes are demanded at some point in the conference, an announcement of the changes can be made verbally at a

plenary session. Following the announcement, the changes can be posted on a single bulletin board in the small office of the conference coordinator.

2. Equipment failure can be orchestrated for effective time lag. Movie projectors can blow fuses, extension cords can be lost, screens can be too small, films can be broken, ventilation in meeting rooms may be inadequate, public-address systems can squeal or be of insufficient wattage, mimeograph machines and electric typewriters can jam, and copy machines may run out of webbing.

3. If the meeting site is some distance from the housing site, the arrangements committee can arrange for charter buses to transport the conference participants between the two points. Appropriate rush-hour scheduling, use of inexperienced drivers, and equipment failures are among the many possibilities for arrangements committees to foster the principles of dynamic inaction.

THE CONFERENCE WRAP-UP

Late in the afternoon of the last day of the conference, the co-chairmen of the discussion groups should report in a plenary session the general conclusions and recommendations of their groups. Properly orchestrated, the final report can be completed about an hour before the conference banquet.[3] If the conferring group is a for-

[3]An international example of this pattern was demonstrated in the Inter-American Conference of the Partners of the Americas held in San Jose, Costa Rica, in 1971. Some of the private-sector probus kept the executive committee of the U. S. branch of the organization in meetings until the final three hours of the conference. Through the use of proxies, the majority position of the executive committee of the U. S. branch proposed that the Latin-American participants in the Inter-American program have less than a fifty-fifty voice in the policies of the program. The U. S. delegates to the conference rejected the U. S. executive committee's recommendations and voted that the Latin Americans should have a fifty-fifty position on the decision-making board. The Latin-American delegates and the majority of the U. S. delegates left the conference thinking that the "partnership of equals concept of the program had been saved. The private-sector probus on the defeated executive committee, however, demonstrated the effectiveness of policy thwartation through the use of the study-committee technique. Months of study, committee meetings, and telephone conversations in the United States resulted in altering the decisions made in San Jose without the concurrence of the Latin-American participants in the program. Gringo jingoism! Policy thwartation by semantical artistry, unilateral mumbling, and minivision tactics.

mal organization, and if elections are required, the elections can be held following the final report. Such timing normally will optimize the opportunities for probus to retain or gain control.

THE CONFERENCE BANQUET

With the major effort in behalf of dynamic inaction having been completed, the probus should move into the banquet session with maximum cordiality. They will have undoubtedly succeeded in preserving the grand old principles that have served so well for generations, and they should use the banquet session as an instrument for keeping the activists within the orbit of putteristic dialoguing. The banquet should be one that limits the speech-making to fifteen minutes and gives the balance of time to food, refreshments, and entertainment.

THE CONFERENCE CONCLUSIONS

Whatever else the final report of the conference may include, it is imperative that it state that the conference just concluded was fruitful and opened new insights into the problems of the industry, system, or agency. Finally, there must be a forthright call for another conference to be held in the future, and a conference planning committee should be appointed.

Principles
of Decision
Postponement

nterface avoidance and decision postponement are opposite sides of the same bureaucratic coin. They constitute perhaps the most effective and most congenial hand-maiden to dynamic inaction. The techniques for postponement implementation are limited only by the imagination and the determination of the bureaucrat. The grand old friends of the system, however, are: (1) the committee process, and (2) the clearance mechanisms.

COMMITTEE PROCESS

The use of the study committee can be traced to Adam and Eve and the dialogue between Eve and the serpent as they considered the effect of eating the fruit of the tree that was in the midst of the Garden of Eden. According to some scholars who have given much time to introspective research, the committee process received its next great impetus when "the sons of Noah, after their generations," determined to build a tower that was to reach unto heaven. Informed theologians believe that there was established a committee to study the feasibility of the plan, another committee to select the site, and a third committee to schedule the use of the materials of brick, stone, and mortar. High-level clearance apparently was not given for the project, however, and the committees were disbanded. Action was taken to "confound the language of all the earth."

Thus began man's concern with committees, clearances, and mumbling.

Today, there are very few actions that can be taken that do not involve the functioning of a committee. Every known institutional arrangement through which man works, plays, or worships is bound up in the red thread of the committee process. Program committees, ways and means committees, membership committees, decoration committees, food committees, and on and on. No greater friend hath dynamic inaction than the committee process!

Committees are created in many different forms, but they remain the same basic committee known of old. A political speaker in East Texas once held aloft for a crowd to see a glass jar that contained a large cockroach. To the back of the cockroach had been glued small pieces of chinchilla fur. Though the speaker described his chinchilla in elegant terms, it remained the same cockroach. Today, governmental structure is filled with Presidential task forces and blue-ribbon commissions.

Study committees are the bureaucrat's best instrument to avoid decisions that may add additional work, be embarrassing, or be otherwise undesirable. When public issues are charged with great emotion and danger for the bureacracy, the bureaucratic leadership can simply refer the matter to a study committee. The bureaucrat may not, and usually doesn't, desire any serious recommendations, but he may desire some acceptable method of putting the matter in untroubling suspense until the public clamor dies away. The bureaucrat appointing the committee need not disclose his true purpose to the members of the committee, but he can use the committee members to: (1) give public attention to the sincerity of his concern; (2) serve as a buffer between the bureaucrat and the public; and (3) orchestrate the time lag for maximized decision postponement and interface avoidance.

In the Federal system of the government today, there are approximately 850 study groups that are effective instruments of the postponement pattern. Such groups may evolve into temporary commissions. The temporary commissions may evolve into permanent agencies or bureaus within agencies, and the priority nature of a problem may be translated into a long-range priority program.

Committees may function through a series of subcommittees, but the best opportunity for a bureaucrat to gain postponement experience is through an assignment with inter-agency or inter-departmental committees. Representatives on such committees obviously cannot make commitments for their respective agencies without consultation with the agency leadership. This offers a fine opportunity for decision prolongation. When a tentative decision is finally reached, of course, it should be couched in terms of "agreement in principle." Such a move provides an opportunity for the bureaucrat to maneuver for optimal status position until the final minute of an inter-agency committee's existence. Properly handled, a bureaucrat may be able to make a lifetime career of an inter-agency committee assignment. While substantive issues may never be dealt with, the bureaucrat will have ample opportunity to speak and write in substantive terms. Such an opportunity for public service is devoutly to be wished.

CLEARANCE MECHANISMS

After study-committee reports are reviewed by review committees, and review committee reports are surveyed by survey committees, the survey committee reports should be coordinated by coordinating committees. The full thrust of orchestrated clearances is to give proper escalation to decision postponement that is the heart of dynamic inaction.

Clearances are basically of two types, direct clearances and sequential clearances. Direct clearances provide some opportunity for decision delay, but there is little opportunity for retractive interfacing. Direct clearances involve a one-to-one relationship without reference to prior clearances by other bureaucrats. For example, if a teacher must have a clearance from the department head to purchase a box of paper clips, and if no other clearances are required, the clearance is a simple and direct clearance.

Another class of direct clearance is exemplified by the case of a filing specialist who needs a new set of dividers for the files. The specialist must obtain the clearance of the office director, the bureau chief, and the assistant comptroller, but none of the three clearances depends on prior clearances by either of the other two clearers. The simple clearee-to-clearer relationship without sequence requirements is a relatively ineffective device for decision postponement.

Sequential clearances are clearances that require a definite order in which clearances must be obtained. For example, an educator in the midwest who wishes to attend a major educational conference in Denver may be required to obtain approval of his travel plans from seven different offices. First, for example, he may be required to obtain clearance from his department head. Second, he must clear with his dean, then his academic vice president. His final clearance on campus may be that of the president of the institution—unless the president decides the comptroller should stamp the travel-request form with a stamp showing that funds are available. The state treasurer may then give his clearance, but all previous clearances are of no avail unless, under statutory requirement, the governor of the state approves and initials the request form.

If the dean is attending another conference in another city, and the professor cannot obtain the dean's signature, he may miss the vital conference because the academic vice president will not approve without the clearance of the dean. If the dean returns in time, of course, the sequence can begin to function again from that point upward.

Fifteen to twenty clearances are common elements of sequential chains in the Pentagon, State Department, and international agencies. Sequential clearances may result in decision postponement for as long as six months, particularly if a general counsel's office is involved.

To prevent hasty decisions, therefore, the probu should collaborate effectively in developing sequential-clearance chains. For the bureaucrat, the greatest danger to sequential devices is to be found in beginning bureaucrats who may not yet understand the system and may either want to reduce the clearances or insist on the use of information copies instead of clearances.

If the *status quo* is to be maintained, and if dynamic inaction is to be given its proper role in interface avoidance and decision postponement, the bureaucrats of the nation must reverently preserve the committee process and clearance mechanisms.

Boldness of irresolution, dynamic inaction, interface avoidance, committee-oriented mumbling, and leadership by sensorship—these are elements of the tapestry that may ultimately serve as the drapery of the couch that we as a nation will draw about us as we lie down to pleasant dreams.

Random Thoughts of a Professional Bureaucrat

Guidelines for
Position Evaluation

hen professional colleagues in other organizations or nonprofessionals from the outside world visit the office of a bureaucrat, they make immediate judgments as to the level in the hierarchy that the host bureaucrat occupies. Status symbols are essentially the same in various types of bureaucracies, but there are institutional variables that may affect client response. The random listing of status symbols provides an opportunity for developing bureaucrats to practice the assessment skills that are a part of the arsenal of bureaucracy.

GUIDELINE PRACTICE SHEET/POSITION EVALUATION

Professional Bureaucrat Senior Level	Professional Bureaucrat Middle Level	Professional Bureaucrat Low Level

Instructions: List the number of the status symbol in the appropriate column to indicate evaluation of the bureaucratic position of a colleague or of a bureaucrat, if rater is a nonpractitioner.

Rating factors/status symbols:
1. Concrete or tile floor
2. Rug on floor
3. Wall-to-wall carpeting
4. Venetian blinds on windows
5. Curtains on windows
6. Drapes on windows
7. Filing cabinets in office
8. No filing cabinets in office
9. Black telephone
10. Call director
11. Small room
12. Large room
13. Offiice with windows

14. Office with windows, no view
15. Office with windows, with view
16. Small desk
17. Large desk
18. Single-occupant office
19. Double-occupant office
20. Multi-occupant office
21. Two or more hard chairs
22. Upholstered chairs
23. No couch
24. With couch
25. No coffee table
26. With coffee table
27. With refrigerator
28. No refrigerator
29. Assigned secretary
30. Secretary from secretary pool
31. Picture prints on wall
32. Original paintings on wall
33. No water pitcher
34. Plastic water pitcher
35. Silver water pitcher
36. Coffee served in paper cups
37. Coffee served in white glass cups
38. Coffee served in china cups with saucer
39. No pen set on desk
40. Plastic pen set on desk
41. Onyx or marble-base pen set on desk
42. Private toilet in office
43. Office located next to noisy toilets
44. Office with no copy machine
45. Office with copy machine

Non-office rating factors (when observable):
1. Access to executive dining room
2. Access to cafeteria
3. Regular passport
4. Official passport
5. Telephone answered with bureaucrat's name
6. Telephone answered with number or "hello"
7. Bust size of secretary, if any (secretary)
8. Assigned parking space
9. No assigned parking space
10. Parking space assigned, parking lot
11. Parking space assigned, within building, distant from door
12. Parking space assigned, within building, close to door
13. Parking space assigned, by name

Sex
and the Bureaucrat

Chapman

SEXUAL FANTASIES PROVIDE WELCOME
CONTRAST TO DYNAMIC INACTION

Publisher's Note: The inhibitions of the author plus intimidation by his family brought a temporary end to his research into the sex life of the bureaucrat. From his extensive collection of raw material, however, the author has made available four unevaluated tables. The manner of data collection and the method of sampling have been classified SECRET by the author. The tables are presented without comment.

ORGANOGRAM FIVE E/EPSILON
Is Sex Necessary?

	Yes	No	Yes, But	No, But	Undecided
Department of State	1	2	7	7	83
Department of the Treasury	2	3	45	45	5
Department of Justice	2	2	86	2	8
Department of the Army	2	2	13	1	82
Department of the Navy	5	3	11	2	79
Department of the Air Force	90	0	2	1	7
Department of Health, Education, and Welfare	18	1	77	2	2
Department of Housing and Urban Development	2	1	1	1	95
Department of Transportation	8	2	46	3	43
Department of Agriculture	18	2	17	13	50
Department of Commerce	20	20	20	20	20
Department of Labor	76	1	2	20	1
Department of the Interior	2	4	3	85	6
Postal Service	93	1	1	4	1
House of Representatives	0	0	0	0	100
Senate	0	0	0	0	100
White House	NR	NR	NR	NR	NR

NR: No Response.

ORGANOGRAM SIX F/ZETA
Why Is Sex Necessary?

	Health	Fun	Duty	Undecided
Department of State	2	1	8	89
Department of the Treasury	2	2	3	93
Department of Justice	3	2	87	8
Department of the Army	2	8	9	81
Department of the Navy	4	12	3	81
Department of the Air Force	2	91	2	5
Department of Health, Education, and Welfare	95	1	3	1
Department of Housing and Urban Development	2	1	1	96
Department of Transportation	12	13	26	49
Department of Agriculture	16	12	18	54
Department of Commerce	25	25	25	25
Department of the Interior	14	47	31	8
Department of Labor	1	2	64	33
Postal Service	2	83	4	11
House of Representatives	0	0	0	100
Senate	0	0	0	100
White House	NR	NR	NR	NR

NR: No Response.

ORGANOGRAM SEVEN G/ETA
When Is Sex Necessary?

	Before End of Calendar Year	Before End of Fiscal Year	Con-ferences	Undecided
Department of State	1	15	1	83
Department of the Treasury	2	2	2	94
Department of Justice	2	94	2	2
Department of the Army	3	12	1	84
Department of the Navy	1	15	1	83
Department of the Air Force	2	65	30	3
Department of Health, Education, and Welfare	2	83	14	1
Department of Housing and Urban Development	1	1	1	97
Department of Transportation	2	45	7	45
Department of Agriculture	1	37	10	52
Department of Commerce	25	25	25	25
Department of Labor	14	23	12	51
Department of the Interior	3	80	9	8
Postal Service	2	4	90	4
House of Representatives	0	0	0	100
Senate	0	0	0	100
White House	NR	NR	NR	NR

NR: No Response.

ORGANOGRAM EIGHT H/THETA
Performance*

	Precise	Casual	Routine	Process Committee	None
Department of State	88	1	3	6	2
Department of the Treasury	18	1	80	1	0
Department of Justice	38	2	42	10	8
Department of the Army	10	8	70	10	2
Department of the Navy	92	1	3	1	3
Department of the Air Force	0	1	49	40	0
Department of Health, Education, and Welfare	44	8	7	40	1
Department of Housing and Urban Development	1	1	2	3	93
Department of Transportation	16	20	39	20	5
Department of Agriculture	12	10	70	4	4
Department of Commerce	20	20	20	20	20
Department of Labor	3	26	22	27	22
Department of the Interior	17	17	63	1	2
Postal Service	2	2	46	40	8
House of Representatives	0	0	50	25	25
Senate	0	0	25	25	50
White House	49	0	1	1	49

*Based on unsolicited reports from Washington's professional corps.

BABY PROBU'S HERITAGE

By the shores of Dirty River,
By the shining Big Potomac,
Stood the wigwam of Noklearance,
Daughter of the Moon, Noklearance,
Dark behind it rose the buildings,
Rose the large and gloomy structures,
Rose the files with locks upon them;
Dull before it beat the waters,
Beat the dull and sluggish waters,
Beat the odorous Big Potomac.
   There the tape-bound old Noklearance
Nursed the little Baby Probu,
Rocked him in his three-tiered in-box,
Bedded soft in forms and memos,
Safely bound with red-tape sinews;
Stilled his driving force by sayings,
"Hush! Or Big Brother will hear thee!"
Lulled him into slumber, singing,
"Yea-and-nay! my little fledgling!
Who is this, that rocks the wigwam?
With great files fills the wigwam?
Yea-and-nay! my little fledgling."
   At the desk on Friday mornings,
Sat the little Baby Probu;
Heard the typing of the memos,
Heard the tapping of the fingers,
Sounds of meetings, words of wonder;
"Minne-wawa!" said the mumblers,
"Let us ponder!" said the dancers.
   Many things Noklearance taught him
Of the words that sing in memos;
Showed him Pentagon, the spender,
Pentagon, with flashy phrases;
Showed the Street Dance of Protesters,
Warriors with their chants and placards,
Marching faraway to nowhere
Through the darkened halls of learning;
Showed the bureaus' road to heaven,
Pathway of the hand, the clearance,
Running straight across the memos,
Crowded with the lines, initials.
   Then the little Baby Probu
Learned from every pro his language,

Learned their names and all their secrets,
How they built their nests in bureaus,
Where they hid themselves in winter,
Tucked away from new appointees,
Called them "Baby Probu's Dancers."
　From all the pros he learned the language,
Learned the charts and all the channels,
How the chieftains built their bureaus,
Where the chieftains hid their errors,
How the bureaus grew so swiftly,
Why the young ones were so timid,
Talked with them whene'er he caught them,
Called them "Baby Probu's Dancers."

Thoughts
on Major Issues

COMPUTERS

Many dedicated bureaucrats have expressed concern that they might one day be replaced by a computer. Probus should not be alarmed by the increasing use of the computer because: (1) it is possible to computerize indecision; (2) the speed of computers cannot match the skill of Peter Principle Bureaucrats in developing longer and more deliberate clearance procedures; and (3) computers can't vote.

POLITICAL DINNERS

Corporate and academic bureaucrats share the target site of department heads who have a quota of "tables" to sell when the political fund-raising dinners are in season. It is the governmental bureaucrat, however, who must carefully weigh the manner of responding to dinner invitations. Political operatives in key positions in the executive branch and in the national political party headquarters maintain accurate records of contributors to political dinners. The records constitute the memory bank of "ours" and "theirs" when a change of administration ultimately comes.

The probus should prodigiously ponder the methods of neutral gearing, but successful techniques should only be shared with intimate friends—in *other* departments. One generally effective method involves being on vacation or on a field trip, attending a conference, or in some other manner being out of the city.

Should a financial contribution be extracted later, the subsequent-to-the-dinner lists of contributors are less accurately recorded in the party's memory bank. As with a change of administration, the most helpful rule is: When in political crosswinds, residuate.

POPULATION CRISIS

The rapid growth of the world's population is a matter of grave concern to most national leaders. Like so many other major issues, however, the solution is readily at hand, but congressional leaders and cabinet officials do not give sufficient attention to the creative recommendations of the nation's probus. The population growth rate could be reduced by 100 percent if a massive research program could be launched for the purpose of finding the means of doubling the human gestation period.

Medical researchers and bureaucrats should be able to develop the plan by which Mother Nature could be taught the principles of governmental programming, clearance techniques, and policy implementation. If these principles can be orchestrated in a series of collaborative study committees, the pregnancy period can be extended a minimum of an additional nine months.

WOMEN'S LIBERATION

Bureaucrats who support the bureaucrats' liberation movement should give moral support to the women's liberation efforts. There is, however, a basic philosophical problem confronting senior probus. If probus should support efforts to eliminate the designation of marital status in salutations through the use of Ms. instead of Miss or Mrs., they should also support efforts to eliminate the designation of sex in salutations. Therefore, instead of Ms., the probus of the nation should use the salutation of Mm. Not only does Mm eliminate the designation of sex, it also possesses the tonal qualities for optimized mumbling. Such a change in salutations would also help those who do not know the sex of persons being addressed in written communication or in face-to-face communication. Since it is increasingly difficult to determinate the sex of people by their appearance, the bureaucrats' golden rule of life can be brought into play: When in doubt, mumble.

TEARS AS A MOTIVATIONAL INSTRUMENT

Tears have long been an effective device for altering decisions already made or in process of being made. Efficiency reports, vacation schedules, work loads, and other important factors have been affected by the appropriate orchestration of tears. The effectiveness of tears is greatly increased when the producer is a female, and the effectiveness is almost 100 percent if the female is: (1) well-endowed, and (2) wears plunging necklines or short miniskirts. Bald-headed professors seeking promotion from the assistant to the associate-professor rank, or paunchy GS-7's seeking a GS-9 position in the governmental sphere may be less than 100 percent effective. Of course, as the women's liberation movement gains ground and more senior probus are involved in the personnel problems, the percentage of effectiveness may be modified. Tears still tend to look better on miniskirts than on vests.

OFFICE PARTIES

When in trouble, delegate.

HOW A CORPORATION CAN SPEND ITS WAY OUT OF BANKRUPTCY

Bureaucrats in management have a responsibility to themselves to devote company time and resources to improve the corporate enjoyment curve. The fringe benefits of management should be increased at a constant growth rate until productivity and profits are negatively affected. At such a point, the company's creditors and stockholders may become troublesome and somewhat meddlesome.

As the first draft of bankruptcy papers is being written by the company's attorneys, management should take a few steps that will provide short-term funds for a major survival program. For example, the fleet of limousines and executive airplanes may be reduced, leased hotel suites and golf club memberships around the world may be suspended temporarily, and company yachts may be kept in port. Token reductions in salaries may be volunteered. Proper orchestration by forward-looking management may result in financial assistance from unions and the area's business leadership. With funds in hand, management can launch its program of survival spending.

Survival teams should be developed with the help of paid organizers. The teams should include the leadership of the state and local members of commerce, union leaders, Jaycees, bankers, mayors, clergymen, publishers, and editors—and anyone else who understands the principles of fulcrum placement. Money should be spent generously in sending waves of flights to Washington in search of government understanding. This can be in the form of new government contracts, emergency grants, tax forgiveness, money advances on programmed over-runs, and other helpful governmental response.

All team activities, of course, should be coordinated through the congressional delegation.

Survival expenditures of this type can be helpful when the inputs are appropriately orchestrated. It should be understood, however, that massive spending over a number of years must be a part of the corporate thrust, because such spending creates the image of corporate giantism that must be preserved "in the national interest." When the crisis has been passed, the proper attention can again be given to the enjoyment curve.

LEADERSHIP THROUGH SENSORSHIP

Chiefs of state as well as working bureaucrats have learned that leadership is not necessarily made of conviction and forceful persuasion, but leadership involves skillful movement with the crowd. Crowd values that can be the clue for national leadership are best ascertained through a system of sensorship. Polls, demonstrations, boycotts, news feedback, opinions of taxi drivers, and mail-weighing are effective targets for sensing the ebb and flow of crowd attitudes. (Weighing mail refers, of course, to physical volume and weight, and has nothing to do with weight of arguments.) The leader, therefore, is the one who can proclaim with volume and move with bold resolution—as soon as he senses from the crowd the direction in which he is supposed to lead.

Glossary
of Terms
and Phrases

SENIOR BUREAUCRAT IS READY
AT ALL TIMES FOR DYNAMIC INACTION

Acabu (Pronounced: *ackaboo*) An academic bureaucrat. A specialized class of professional bureaucrat (probu).

Bureaucrat A person dedicated to the optimization of the creative *status quo*. Professional bureaucrats employ committee processes, use clearance mechanisms, and apply the principles of dynamic inaction for the purpose of effecting decision postponement and interface avoidance. Normally characterized by skill in mumbling, pondering, and delegating. Originally, bureaucrat was a term applied to employees of government bureaus, but today a bureaucrat may be found in every type of human endeavor. For some people, bureaucracy is a religion.

Bureaucratic Movement, The (Also known as The BM). The flow of bureaucracy from Washington to other parts of the nation. Known in Washington as The Movement; known in most of the country as The BM of Washington.

Dittoanalysis The process by which echosultants arrive at conclusions previously determined.

Fuzzistic Planned or programmed fuzziness as distinguished from haphazard or accidental fuzziness.

Linear mumbling The translocation of tonal patterns that reflect the bold irresolution of a speaker. Not distinguishable in word forms.

Memo retraction shredder Specialized equipment for permanently retracting the communicative thrust of memoranda and other documents by a shredding process.

Movement, The The flow of bureaucracy from Washington to other parts of the nation. Known in Washington as The Movement, but known in other parts of the nation as The Bureaucratic Movement or The BM.

Mumblistic Planned or programmed mumbling as distinguished from unintentional mumbling. viz., a mumblistic speaker.

Obscurate Bureaucratic verb form; to preserve bureaucratic obscurity. Obscuration is similar to residuation in its outward manifestation, but it differs in the bureaucratic level at which it is used. Bureaucrats of all levels may residuate but normally only bureaucrats at lower levels obscurate. See: **Residuate.**

Polibu (Pronounced *polyboo*). Political bureaucrat; a specialized type of professional bureaucrat (probu).

PPB Peter Principle Bureaucrat. The highest level of probuistic success. The PPB designation is the Ph.D. of bureaucracy.

Probu (Pronounced *proboo*) A professional bureaucrat; one who has accepted the principle of dynamic inaction as a life style.

Probuistic Purposeful bureaucratic planning by a professional bureaucrat. Bureaucratic processes may be beautiful, but also may be accidental. Probuistic processes, or probuisms, must be planned by a professional bureaucrat.

Profundicator A person skilled in translating simple concepts into multi-phasic patterns of semantical infusions characterized by minimal disambiguation.

Putteristic Planned or programmed puttering as distinguished from unplanned or random puttering.

Residuate Bureaucratic verb form for approximating a residual profile. A residual profile is the lowest of low profiles, and is widely used in governmental agencies, corporations, and educational institutions during changes of administration. Residuum-related.

Twiddlism A short radius referral. Employee A refers a memo to Employee B. Employee B returns the memo to Employee A. Twiddlisms may be developed in series.

Twiddlistic Planned or programmed twiddlisms.

Vertical Mumbling Maximized utilization of word strings; made more effective when developed with multi-syllable words that possess tonal qualities for optimacy of projected resonance.